The African Guide to

Success In America

By Walter Ray

The African Guide To Success And Prosperity In America

Introduction

This book is written especially for the African immigrant but can be utilized to great advantage by all who read it. It is for those who dream of traveling to The United States of America and starting life anew in "The land of the free and the home of the brave." This phrase, "The land of the free and the home of the brave" is commonly heard in the American media space and is central to the nation and to the culture. I will be introducing the reader to aspects of American culture throughout the book.

The book is also written with the immigrant in mind who has already migrated to the United States and has not yet figured out the critical things which can lead him or her to a more successful life. This book will reveal ideas, plans, concepts and strategies that will enable the reader to gain a greater insight into specific areas of American life and culture. It will enable the reader to become successful in a short amount of time.

Trial and error are two of life's most common learning tools. Or as some would call it, "The school of hard knocks." The problem with the school of hard knocks is that it may well take one a lifetime to learn the strategies needed and methods

The African Guide To Success And Prosperity In America

of operation required for making a successful life. In the U.S. another commonly heard remark is, "If I'd only known fifteen or twenty years ago what I know now!" For the reader, if this book is read and understood it can take that fifteen or twenty years of hard knocks and give it back, with interest. The Bible says, "With all thy getting, get first an understanding." So for all who take the time to read **The African Guide To Success And Prosperity In America** and understand the ideas, plans, concepts and strategies, I can say with certainty that you will have a huge head start on the path to financial independence and success in a new life, in The United States of America.

There are a thousand and one things that the immigrant does not know but needs to know, and the sooner they do know, the better positioned they'll be to take full advantage of all the opportunities that America has to offer. I am a descendant of Mother Africa. Some of my ancestors were taken during the days of the transatlantic slave trade. I am writing this book with the aim of helping those present day Africans who are coming to America by choice and not by force. The book will help you if you take it seriously. Study it. Understand it. It will help you more if you use it not just for personal gain and benefit, but also use it to reach out and reach back to help your family, friends, and those around you. We say in America that God helps those who help themselves. But we

The African Guide To Success And Prosperity In America

also realize that no one achieves great success in life without the help and support from someone or some ones along the way. Marcus Garvey coined the phrase, "Up you mighty nation, you can accomplish what you will!" It is my sincere hope that this book will help to inspire a mighty nation to rise up, inside and outside of Mother Africa for the benefit of us all.

The African Guide To Success And Prosperity In America

Dedication

This book is dedicated to my African ancestors from the lands and tribes that through DNA it has been revealed to me. Namely: the Igbo from Nigeria, the Hausa, the Brong from Ghana, the Bamoun from Cameroon along with several other tribes and groups. You didn't come by choice but by force. Nevertheless, we your descendants are here and your spirit lives and breathes through us even when we are unaware.

The African Guide To Success And Prosperity In America

Chapter One

The First Key:

Living Below Your Means

One of the most important lessons to learn in order to achieve financial success, and in the process accumulate wealth, and the one that takes the most discipline is learning to live not within one's means, but to live beneath one's means. This strategy is especially difficult in the United States because the culture is so committed to consumption, and some would say over consumption. Americans are conditioned early on to spend money on items that they need, but more importantly they are conditioned to spend big money on things that they *want,* but don't really need. Consumer purchasing is the mechanism that turns the wheel that powers the U.S. economy.

The U.S. has one of the most advanced and modern economies in the entire world. The latest in consumer goods, be they fashions (clothing and jewelry), automobiles of every make and model, the latest technology in flat screen TV's, video

The African Guide To Success And Prosperity In America

cameras, computers, laptop or desktop, projectors and all sorts of electronic goods are constantly paraded before the eyes and ears of the consuming and eager public. One can hardly turn on the TV, listen to the radio, or read a magazine or newspaper without being bombarded with sights and sounds of the latest gadgets and gadgetry.

The temptation to consume is probably greater no place on God's green earth than it is in North America. Anything and everything your imagination could possible conjure up is already there and awaiting your arrival. It's there, it's available and it comes with a price. Because the United States is a highly developed country the cost of living is high. These cost include cars, rents, mortgages, food, clothes, you name it, you claim it and you pay for it.

In spite of the high cost of living in the United States as compared to Ghana, West Africa and the developing world, there are ways around the obstacles of high prices and great temptations. This is the first key and maybe the most important key to financial independence and success in America. It too comes with a price and the price you pay for this key is great discipline! Living not within one's means, but living beneath one's means! Let me clarify exactly what I'm speaking of. If a person earns say $20,000 a year but spends $25,000 to $30,000 it means they are living above their means.

The African Guide To Success And Prosperity In America

It may come as a surprise to some, but in the U.S. this is not hard to do. If one earns 40,000 U.S. dollars a year but spends 60,000 U.S. dollars a year, it means they too are living above their means. The same is true for the one who earns 100,000 U.S. dollars a year but spends 150,000 U.S. dollars. Yes they too are guilty of living above their means. This is standard practice in America and closer to the status quo than you may think.

If you've never lived in the western world the thought may cross your mind, how can a person earn 20,000 dollars a year and spend 30,000 dollars that same year or maybe spend more than 30,000 dollars that same year? It may sound like a trick question. It is not. The answer is credit. In the U.S. credit is available to most people and it is fairly easy to obtain. In fact, credit is one of the pillars that hold up the American economy. If consumption turns the wheel, then credit is the grease that allows the wheel to turn. But like I mentioned earlier, it comes with a price. Depending on your *creditworthiness* it can be extremely high.

Now let's get back to living with ones means. Take those earlier examples. The ones who earn $20,000, $40,000 and $100,000 a year respectfully. If they spend exactly what they earn it means they are living within their means. One can either live above their means, within their means or beneath their means. Believe it or not the easiest

The African Guide To Success And Prosperity In America

option is to live above one's means. The reason it's easy to live above your means is because of easy access to credit, plus the fact that it doesn't require any discipline on your part. In a country like the United States of America, that has every consumer good imaginable, it is very easy to spend all that you earn and then some. Once you've exhausted your pay along comes easy credit and you go into debt by spending what you don't have, in order to have your wants piled on top of your needs.

The key as I've stated earlier is to live beneath one's means (income), in order to achieve financial independence and build wealth. The reason is simple to understand but for most Americans it is hard to implement. When one lives beneath their means (they spend less than they make), they'll have disposable income that they can use to invest in any number of profitable ways. Spending less than one earns requires tremendous discipline, especially in America where the beck and call of the marketplace is stronger than anywhere on earth.

I use to sell life insurance for a company called Western and Southern in Kansas City Kansas. My immediate manager was a middle aged white man name Jack. He was about twenty years my senior and lived in a relatively small town in Kansas, not far from Kansas City. Now Jack and I were not the best of friends. As a matter of fact I really didn't like him and could tell his feelings towards me were mutual. Even though I didn't much like Jack, I gained a degree of knowledge and insight from my association with him that went far beyond selling life insurance.

As we traveled around Kansas City, Kansas selling insurance and collecting premiums, Jack would talk to me about his outside investments. He'd tell me about his treasury bills, other bonds he held, his certificate of deposits (CD's) and when they'd mature, a little about stocks and a smattering of real estate investments. Most of Jack's outside investments were conservative in nature, meaning he wasn't going to make a huge return in a short amount of time, but he wasn't going to lose anything either. Slow and steady was the course Jack had staked out for his road to financial independence and wealth accumulation. This was the mid 1980's and Jack earned an average income from selling life insurance. Even at the managerial level I doubt that Jack made over $30,000 a year.

One day as we were riding doing our insurance business, Jack was telling me about when this CD or that savings bond was due to mature. Then he told me that everything that he buys, he buys with cash. He said that when it's time to purchase a new car he takes $10,000 to $12,000 in cash and buys it outright. Jack said that the only thing he buys on credit is a house. He said the mortgage allows him certain advantages when he files his taxes. The tax advantages help to offset the interest built into the house note. Then he said something that blew my twenty something year old mind. Jack said I don't pay interest, I get paid interest!

With all thy getting, get first an understanding. That statement from Jack about not paying interest but getting paid interest put it all together for me and gave me a profound understanding on how to live life to the fullest based on sound financial principal. Because Jack didn't live off of credit (and in debt), he was able to pay cash for everything and invest his disposal income into financial instruments that *paid him interest.* Then Jack said that he made more money on his investments than he made selling insurance!

Jack had gained financial freedom. He'd gained his financial freedom by understanding and following sound wealth building strategies that are available to us all. They are simple and easy to understand. They require sacrifice and huge discipline. I grew up during the Civil Rights Movement and something I always heard repeated was the statement, "Freedom ain't free!" Neither is financial independence and wealth creation. One will have to pay the price. The price is well worth the sacrifice. If Jack's job failed or if *he decided* to quit for any number of reasons, his investments earned him enough money to pay all his bills and allow him to continue to live life on his terms, worry free.

In my humble estimation Jack wasn't any smarter than the average man or woman. His advantage over the average person was in his basic understanding about conservative investments, and the discipline to stick to a regular savings and investing routine over a considerable period of time. He could proudly say with truth that his investments paid him more than his job because he lived beneath his means. He spent less than he made! With that simple understanding and the application of a basic principal he gained financial independence and freedom from want or worry.

This approach to wealth creation is available to anyone with the discipline to do without short term pleasures in order to have long term gain. It must be said that the less money one earns on their job, the more difficult it will be to live below one's means. Nevertheless, difficult though it may be, it can still be done. Great accomplishments call for great sacrifices. In the United States of America, the national legal minimum wage as of the writing of this book is somewhere around $7.50 per hour. That may seem like a hefty sum for one who has never lived in the western world. Believe me, it is not. But I will argue that even on a minimum wage a person

The African Guide To Success And Prosperity In America

can find ways to save and invest a small portion of their income while living debt free.

It may mean working two jobs. One full time, the other part time. It may mean quitting smoking and thereby saving your life along with somewhere in the neighborhood of $160.00 a month! It could mean that you'll need to cook all your meals at home and not go out to restaurants for the next few years. Maybe you'll need to get a bus pass and ride public transportation, while doing without your own personal automobile, at least for the time being. It could mean living in a studio, rather than in a one or two bedroom apartment. Maybe you'll have to share a house or apartment with family members or friends until you get in a stronger financial position.

Here's the point. There are many sacrifices and choices that one can make in their personal life to put them in a better long term financial position. There are many things that one can do without. I like to call them nonessentials. By sacrificing the nonessentials you'll be in a position to create a savings plan, a plan for financial independence and wealth creation.

The task will in no way be an easy one. The temptations of living in the U.S. of A can overwhelm the most disciplined of people. The latest pair of designer jeans, the newest sneakers,

The African Guide To Success And Prosperity In America

the just released CD's and DVD's, and the cutest, hottest autos at the car shows will all be calling your name and begging for all that you have, and even asking you for what you don't have. It's here, it's available. You can have it if you want it. It will take all the will power at your disposal to turn it down.

The thing to understand is that you won't be denying yourself the finer things in life forever. What you will be doing is saying no to short term gratification so that you'll be able to enjoy long term financial success and accumulate real wealth. You have a clear choice. Live your life under stress with ever increasing debts and worry, or make the sacrifices early so that you can create the kind of lasting wealth that will give you peace of mind, freedom of movement, and opportunities to do as you please in innumerable ways.

I challenge you to live below your means and save as much as you can for ten years. Invest the savings so that you are getting interest or some other kind of legitimate return on your money. If you can save, invest, live debt free, below your means for ten years, by the end of that ten year period you will have accumulated enough cash, stocks, bonds, etc to be well on your way to living a financially independent life. By then you should be in a strong position to start your own business *without* going into debt.

The African Guide To Success And Prosperity In America

Maybe your goal is to ship a container of second hand goods to Tema, Ghana. Or maybe you want to ship construction equipment or even automobiles to Africa or Central America. Maybe your goal is to start investing in real estate in Africa or America, or both places. Some may be blessed to have found a career that satisfied their souls and have decided that they like the investment game. For those lucky few the thing to do will be to keep on working in your chosen professions and keep watching your investments and money grow. Maybe one day you'll end up like my coworker Jack, making more money from your investments than you make from your job.

Key Number 1

More In Than Out!

You may have already guessed that the first key to financial independence and wealth building is to have more coming into your pocket than leaves your pocket. You need to be getting more money than you're spending, week after week, month after month and year after year. It's a simple concept. A third grader can understand it. To fully appreciate the concept, the light in your mind needs to be activated.

The African Guide To Success And Prosperity In America

It's like being lost inside a pitch black building and stumbling along until someone turns on the lights. When the light is turned on you can see everything clearly. When the light comes on you can move through the building without stumbling and with full confidence. It's easy to move around once the light comes on. But living under crushing debt and never having enough to make ends meet is like stumbling around and injuring yourself in the dark.

When the light comes on you'll stop spending more than you earn. When the light comes on you'll be on your way to wealth and financial freedom. When the light comes on you'll be a good example and a role model that family, friends, neighbors and others can look to for guidance. When the light comes on you won't be asking for a helping hand, you'll be giving a helping hand. I'll close by quoting a verse from The Bible. "Put not your light under a bushel basket where it cannot be seen but put it up on a hill where it can be seen by many." It's a loose quote, but you know the chapter and verse or at least the gist of it.

Chapter 2

Key 2

Education and Training

The United States of America is a highly educated, sophisticated and technologically advanced society. Compared to the continent of Africa and many other places in the world, she is light years ahead in most every human endeavor. She has numerous hospitals, clinics and medical facilities in just about every town and city. Most if not all are equipped with the most up to date and modern medical equipment and the latest technologies that the world has to offer. MRI and CAT scans are easily obtained. X-ray machines, blood pressure monitors and diagnostic equipment that run the full gamut are in every hospital and many clinics.

The African Guide To Success And Prosperity In America

When it comes to education, there are no schools under trees and have not been for the past 100 years or so. Even in the poorest of communities, there are school buildings that are heated in the cold winter months and cooled in the heat of summer. A *free* public school education is a right that all are entitled to receive. They don't have school fees or associated cost to attend. Books are supplied to each and every student. Even in poor districts, with so called failing schools, a motivated student can excel with hard work and sacrifice and go on to college. They can accomplish whatever goal they have set for themselves and achieve their dreams.

The university system is nationwide. There are numerous fully accredited universities and two year community colleges in just about every city. Most small towns have colleges either in them or in a nearby town or city. The educators and support staff are well paid and paid on time. The systems in the American society work efficiently, effectively and they work right on time. It is unheard of for the government or whatever agency is in charge to not pay their employees for two, three, or six months, due to lack of funds, corruption or just plain lack of concern for its employees.

America leads the world in most human endeavors. They pride themselves on being the forerunners in science, technology, education

The African Guide To Success And Prosperity In America

(especially at the university level), automobile manufacturing, sending men and women into outer space and bringing them back alive, military might and economic domination on a global scale. She also takes pride in and bragging rights by winning more gold, silver and bronze medals at every world Olympic event than any other nation. She's a world leader in fields too numerous to mention.

To qualify for leadership in today's world one needs to be educated and/or highly trained. This goes for the individual as well as the nation. In order to gain monetary success in America, one needs to have a quality education and lacking a sound quality education, one should be skilled and trained to a high degree, in a specific field that pays well and offers the individual some sense of personal satisfaction. One can be employed in an occupation that pays well but that doesn't mean they like it. They may hate the job they do, and hate going to work every day. If this happens to be the case, as it is for many, then regardless of how much money one earns, one can't quite claim the title "successful." If you hate the work you do, it creates stress on a daily basis that can and probably will lead to ill health, failed or failing relationships, and dissatisfaction with your overall quality of life.

This is where the beauty of a good, well rounded education as opposed to a trade or skill that pays well comes into play. With the accredited university degree, one has more vertical, as well as horizontal mobility and freedom of movement, into and out of a wider variety of jobs and positions. Each individual must make their own choices, but the more insight one has into the possibilities and outcomes of those decisions before they embarked upon the path, the wiser decision they can make. A word to the wise, "One is never too old to learn."That includes returning to school! It's never too late.

In Ghana and I imagine on the entire continent of Africa, illiteracy is common and widespread. In the United States, if one is unable to read, understand what they've read, write legibly and do basic mathematics, they will have a difficult time surviving, let alone getting ahead in life. If this is the case for any immigrant, they will need to swallow their pride, admit what they lack and determine a course that will allow them to gain what they don't have, which is a formal education.

The good news is that in America there are opportunities for adult education that are free and readily available. There's an education certificate commonly referred to as the G.E.D., which stands for General Equivalency Degree. It's available for people of high school age who may have dropped out of school before graduating. It's also available for adults of any age who don't have a high school diploma. With a G.E.D. one is qualified to enroll in college, as well as in technical and trade schools. It's also a help, and in many cases a requirement for most basic entry level positions.

In The United States of America one needs to be self motivated because the competition for jobs and advancement is real serious. Opportunities abound but one has to be prepared to take full advantage as they arise. Education is a sure fire way to prepare for your life so that you can capitalize on all that the modern world has to offer.

It's also important for the immigrant parent, or parents to be able to motivate their children to strive for excellence and high standards in school. There will be many temptations for the African child and if the parent is unable to see clearly the culture and its drawbacks, they will not be able to steer the child through the hazards that lie in wait for the misguided among us.

Chapter Three
Staying Debt Free

Staying debt free is much easier said than done, especially in the United States. The main reason that people in the United States find it extremely difficult to live a debt free life, is because of the easy availability of credit. On the contrary, in Africa, credit is hardly available to the average person, especially to the poor person with little to no education and no collateral. If it's available at all it comes with very high interest rates, often hovering around 35 to 40 percent! In Africa, God willing, the poor do find ways to get micro loans to start something small, or to finance one thing or the other on a very small scale. The situation in America is vastly different, even for the poor.

For the most part, credit is available for all! One has the opportunity to establish credit fairly easily in America. As long as you have a verifiable job you can build credit. Verifiable means a job that the credit agencies can verify. They have to be able to see that you are working for a registered

The African Guide To Success And Prosperity In America

company and that your employer deducts taxes from your earnings, and pays those taxes to the I.R.S and local tax collecting authorities. Once you've been on the job for a year or two you'll be in a position to start applying for a credit card. MasterCard and Visa are the two most often used and accepted worldwide. You might receive credit applications in the mail before you even think about applying for credit. The point here is to understand the pitfalls of having easy access to credit.

Once credit is established, people tend to use it for everything imaginable. Some of the common things people use credit for are what we call the *big ticket items*. The largest credit purchases that most Americans make are the purchases of houses and automobiles. In Ghana and I imagine throughout Africa, when people build houses, they do so with whatever resources (money) they've been able to save. They build as they go. It may take three years, it may take ten years. Be that as it may, they spend the money they have on hand or from their businesses to build and buy as they go. Very few people in America are in a position to pay cash for a late model automobile and even less so to build or buy a house. The American economy is built largely on credit. Credit is the oil that greases and turns the economic wheel.

Big ticket items like houses, major home improvements, and automobiles are usually

The African Guide To Success And Prosperity In America

purchased by way of mortgages and loans from banks and other financial institutions. Credit cards like MasterCard and Visa are generally used for smaller purchases. Things like clothes, shoes, dinner out with the family and friends, hotel stays, fuel for the car or truck, automobile maintenance, vacations and a host of everyday purchases are oftentimes put on MasterCard or Visa.

So yes credit is indeed available and easy to access for most Americans. The problem lies in the cost that is associated with the easy acquisition of credit. There is no such thing as something for nothing, or like we like to say, there's no free lunch in America. Easy credit comes with a high price, especially for the poor. For the person establishing credit for the first time, interest rates can be pretty high. The rate of interest is the amount of money in percentage terms that the borrower pays back to the creditor who makes the loan. The interest is the amount the borrower pays back to the creditor that is in addition to the amount of the initial loan.

Each time you make a purchase of any amount using your credit card, you'll be charged interest on the amount that has been charged. Let's take as an example that one goes to the gas station and purchases fuel for the automobile, than travels to the grocery store to buy groceries for the week. Let's say the total spending for the day came to $100. For argument's sake, let's say the interest on

The African Guide To Success And Prosperity In America

their MasterCard is 16%. That means at the end of the month when the bill is due to be paid, they'll have to pay the $100 for the fuel and the groceries, and they'll also have to pay an additional $16 for the interest charged by MasterCard for the privilege of using *their* money.

Now here is the tricky part and where the real problem begins. Your credit card company will not require that you pay the entire balance off at the end of the month when the bill comes due. They'll instead send you a bill stating the full amount due, but there will also be a section of the bill that says you need not pay the entire amount. Rather it will say you must pay at least a minimum amount that is something less than the total amount due. In other words, instead of demanding the full amount due at the end of each month they'll give you the option of paying a fraction of the total bill.

Let's say MasterCard says that the minimum amount you can pay on the $100 balance is $15. That means that you can pay the $15 or any amount over the $15 up to the full balance of $116. Say you decide to pay $45 toward the full amount due of $116. This leaves you a balance of $71 due for the following month. Next month instead of charging $100 on your credit card you charge $250. Now you owe $250 plus the $71 from last month, which leaves you owning a balance of $321. But that doesn't include the accumulated interest from the present month. Add the same 16% to the new balance of $321 and you get a total bill at the end of the second month for $372.36. So instead of paying $16 in interest payments, you are now paying $51.36 in interest for the privilege of using someone else's money.

Let's pay this out till the end of the year. Let's assume you get your credit card debt up to $500 and are determined to not allow it to go beyond that point. If the interest rate on your credit card is 16% that would mean that you'd be paying $80 per month every month of the year in interest payments alone. In every twelve month period you'll pay $960 in interest payments. That's the interest payments on just one credit card. (That's just about enough to buy a plot of land in Ghana!) Many Americans, if not most Americans, have three, four and five credit cards. Some have more than five! The interest payments on your credit cards are separate from your interest payments on your house note and car notes. They too come with built in rates of interests.

When this credit situation gets out of control, and for many people it does get out of control, it can cause the kind of stress that leads to ill health, both mental and physical. A friend of mine who has had a history of difficulty when it comes to managing her finances and credit, told me

The African Guide To Success And Prosperity In America

that her mother (may she rest in peace), said to her, "debt can make the mind unbalanced!"

When a person gets so deep into debt that all they are working for is to pay off past bills and accumulated debt, it can leave them in a state of near insanity. Now they go to work to just pay bills. They are working to pay for things that they purchased last year and the years before. They have no money to invest, no money to save. If they decide they'd like to return to school to upgrade their skills and knowledge, they can't afford it. If the job becomes unbearable for any number of reasons, they can't quit because the past debt has a stranglehold on them and the bills *have* to be paid. Strangers will call their house before they get up in the morning and after they go to bed for the night. If they become late in their bill payments harassing phone calls will become the order of the day. The strangers will go so far as calling the person's friends and relatives asking questions about the person who is late on their bills.

When one goes into debt in America and falls behind in payments they can't even keep it a secret. It's like the world knows your business. It even gets so bad for some people that instead of using their earnings to pay off their debts, they borrow more money by way of more credit cards and use the new borrowed money to pay off the old

The African Guide To Success And Prosperity In America

debts, and in the process create more debt and a deeper hole to dig out from under.

If one falls too far behind in their car payments, the automobile dealer whom one purchased the auto from in the first place will repossess the vehicle. The person will be asleep at night, getting their required rest so that they can go to work the next day and when they come out to leave for work in the morning, they discover that their car is missing. Unbeknown to them, the dealer who sold them the car has sent someone to pick it up. It's called repossessing the vehicle. On top of repossessing the vehicle, the dealer will still be demanding full payment for the vehicle! If getting their money means taking you to court, by all means that's what they'll do.

The same methods apply to your house if you fall behind on your payments. If you fall behind by more than two months on your home mortgage payment, your mortgage company will file court papers against you that will allow them to begin the process of foreclosing on your property. This means that you'll be given a certain number of days to vacate the property. The sheriff will be sent to your house with a notice to vacate the premises. He'll nail or otherwise attach the notice to the front of your house for all to see. If you fail to vacate the premises by the date on the notice, he'll return, along with others. The group of them will come into

The African Guide To Success And Prosperity In America

your home whether you are there or not, and they'll put everything you own on the curb by the street.

If it gets to this point there'll be nothing that you can do. If you attempt to resist, the police will be called and they'll haul you off to jail. If you've not made plans to have a truck there when the sheriff comes to take your things away it could really spell trouble. If you leave while your things are still on the curb the people in the neighborhood may well come by like it's Christmas and steal everything you own. It can be a real nightmare.

Debt can make the mind unbalanced! It can be painful and embarrassing. Nevertheless, there is a viable alternative. Like they say, "There is more than one way to skin a cat." That other way, that better alternative is to live a debt free life, at least as much as possible. Living debt free is harder than one may think, especially in a society where everyone around you seems to have so much more than you have.

In the U.S. we have another saying that applies to what we are talking about. It's called, "Keeping up with the Joneses." In practical terms it means that if the neighbors buy a new 50 inch flat screen TV set, you feel like you've got to go out and buy one just as big and just as nice. Keeping up with the Joneses. If they buy a new car, you feel like you should be able to buy a new car too.

The African Guide To Success And Prosperity In America

Keeping up with the Joneses. If your cousin's husband takes her on vacation on a cruise ship, you think your husband should be able to take you on a cruise also. Keeping up with the Joneses is one sure way to create a world of trouble, and a sure way to become a slave to debt and worry.

The way forward to financial success, peace of mind, and the good life is through the cultivation of the habit of living below your means. You need to spend less than you make so that you are able to build a healthy stash of cash. That way you'll be able to pay cash for every item of necessity and even those luxury items like vacations, jewelry, concerts, and the likes thereof. This takes us back to the ideas expressed in chapter one.

The temptations will be great to buy things that you can't afford, with credit that seems easy to obtain, but the cost in the long run is to trade freedom for slavery. You'll be like many poor nations in Africa (and now even European Countries) who are so indebted to The International Monetary Fund and World Bank that all they can do is service the interest on the loans that those institutions have made to them. They have no money left to invest in roads, schools, health care, sewage systems, sanitation or economic development. They pay the debt and the nation suffers. In fact they are so indebted that all they can

The African Guide To Success And Prosperity In America

manage to pay is the interest on the debt, while the principle stares them down like a hungry dog looking at a bone. This is the same reality for many in America. For those who are living in the dark corridors of debt, the American dream can turn into the American nightmare.

The wise and disciplined ones live within and even below their means, so that they are able to invest their disposal income into stocks, bonds, mutual funds, treasury bills, certificates of deposit, real estate, and business ventures that can bring them untold wealth. Some are even able to build real estate empires back in the lands of their birth. An African immigrant in the United States who earns a modest living can easily have enough disposable income to build a nice family house in their home country. With a modest income in the United States they could do any number of ventures, including but not limited to building a hotel/guess house, open a nightclub, create a sizeable farm, start an import/export business or even develop an entire estate. The key is staying out of debt!

Chapter Four

Attitude: The Science of Getting Along With Others

I attended Central High School in Kansas City, Missouri. From time to time I'd stop in the counselor's office. Counselors were available in the schools to provide academic guidance for the students who were motivated enough to seek out there advice. On the wall in the guidance counselor's office hung a plaque that read, "Attitude determines altitude." In other words, a person's attitude plays a huge role in determining their success in life, how high they'll soar or how deep they'll sink. Having a positive attitude in life makes the impossible seem possible. A positive attitude in life opens doors that would otherwise be sealed shut. A positive attitude in life has the power to open the heart of strangers and gain their support for your many endeavors in life.

The African Guide To Success And Prosperity In America

Conversely, a negative attitude in life can turn the hearts and minds of strangers, and even family and friends against you. When it comes to family and friends, maybe they won't turn against you because of your negative attitude but they'll surely have no pleasure in seeing you coming.

A lifelong negative attitude can even lead to your own demise, especially as it relates to your overall health. The negative mind and nasty attitudes can be a poison factory directed towards others, with the intent to do harm, but in the final analysis it will end up doing the most harm to the one who harbors the negativity within their own mind and soul. For the African immigrant coming to America, a word of advice and caution. If you've been conditioned by environment or culture to look down on those less fortunate and have been accustomed to treating them with less than respect, I urge you to stop it now. If you've been conditioned by environment or culture to react to strangers with a nasty disposition it would be to your advantage to begin the process of retraining your mind and heart before you venture to America.

In The United States of America, the *big man* syndrome is barely noticeable and if it exists at all, it is to a much lesser degree. People in America do not bow or defer to others just because they have more money, education, position or power than someone else. Displays of arrogance, which some

The African Guide To Success And Prosperity In America

interpret as ignorance can lead to unnecessary trouble in America. In America there are plenty of poor people, ones who lack quality education, be they black, white, brown, yellow or red who will not tolerate being disrespected just because they lack the things that others take for granted.

One needs to tread with caution with negative or nasty attitudes in America. The wrong words spoken at the wrong time in the wrong way can lead to quick trouble in America. Not only the wrong words but even the wrong looks can go so far as to get one killed in The United States. Since you can't read a book by its cover it will be best to treat everyone you come into contact with, with the same kind of respect you would want shown to you. It boils down to what The Bible says, "Do unto others as you would have them do unto you."

In October 2011 I was on a flight from Accra, Ghana to Atlanta Georgia in the United States by way of Amsterdam Holland. Half way through the flight to Amsterdam a Ghanaian man who looked to be in his early to mid forties started snapping his fingers and calling out to the flight attendant in the most demeaning kind of way. He was calling out to her as if she were one of his house servants back on the farm. The lady happened to be Caucasian (White). Her reaction was swift and direct. She quickly came face to face with the traveler, putting her face about six inches from his.

The African Guide To Success And Prosperity In America

The flight attendant told the man that his behavior is not and will not be tolerated on this flight! She went on to tell him that he'd better leave that attitude wherever he'd found it because in this world it is unacceptable. The Ghanaian man smiled sweetly, humbled himself and offered the flight attendant a sincere apology. He got his first attitude adjustment before he'd even stepped off the plane.

It's no exaggeration to say that the wrong attitude expressed to the wrong person, at the wrong time can get one killed! A very good lifelong friend of my mine lost one of his in-laws to a senseless act of violence. If my memory serves me correct, the young man was related to his wife by way of marriage. He was a young man in his early 20's. He'd made a quick stop at a convenience store. When he came out of the store a car was parked next to his and there were several young men about his age sitting in the car. From my understanding of what happened, my friend's in-law locked eyes with the occupants of the vehicle a little too long. Had he smiled, or even said hello, he may still be among the living today. But he didn't. He just got in his car and drove off. The occupants in the car next to him drove off behind him. They'd taken his stare as an insult. They drove up on him and opened fire with automatic weapons. My friend's in-law's life was taken in a hail of gunfire over a simple stare.

The African Guide To Success And Prosperity In America

There's no law that says you have to speak to strangers, but one must understand that the American culture in many respects is a culture of violence. Certain areas of the city can be a natural hazard to one's health and even their life. There are a small percentage of young people whose minds are so twisted and mixed up that they can kill a person because they don't like the way they were looked at. They took my friend's look as an insult and it cost him his life.

You may be thinking that this couldn't happen to you. Maybe not. Hopefully not. But what about your children, or the children yet unborn? It may surprise you to see how quickly some of the young immigrant children adapt to the American culture and lifestyle. If you have children that are born in America, most Americans at first glance won't even recognize them as African! As I've just shown, a glance, God forbid, can be all it takes to get one killed.

You'll quickly learn in the United States of America that just because one is poor and non white, doesn't mean that they'll allow themselves to be treated in a rude or demeaning sort of way by people who think they are better than them. I'm not saying that you must be perfect. No one is. No one is in a happy upbeat mood 365 days of the year. We all have our moments. We all have our days when things just don't seem right. We all make mistakes

The African Guide To Success And Prosperity In America

and come short of the glory of God. Nevertheless, it is important to be aware of one's general disposition and attitude towards others. When we cultivate a positive attitude and a pleasing disposition we pray that when we come up short, on our bad days, that God will step in the gap and forgive us our sin, so that the world doesn't bring punishment to bear in the devil's name.

I have another friend whom I met in college at the turn of the 21st century. She's a young lady from Nigeria. When I first met her she'd only been in the U.S. for two months. She was not quite 20 years old. We shared a class together and over the ensuing months I became well acquainted with the young lady. After telling me I was a white man (Africans seem to think all people that are not dark skinned Africans are white people), she told me she was mixed. That sounded strange coming from an African because in America we usually associated being mixed with people like Tiger Woods, Halle Berry or Barack Obama. She went on to say that one of her parents was an Ibo and the other parent was a Yoruba. She said in Nigeria that's mixed. I get the feeling that in Nigeria the tribes don't intermarry as frequently as what I've seen happen in Ghana.

I noticed that whenever my African friend entered certain places she'd make it a point to speak to everyone in the room. Not in a how is everyone

The African Guide To Success And Prosperity In America

doing sort of a way, but she would actually go around and speak to them individually, and shake their hands at the same time. She made people's day, by taking the time to involve them in her life in a very personal sort of way.

She's a very classy, well built and good to look at young sister. She's also the granddaughter of a Yoruba Chief who was not just any chief, but one of a certain degree of wealth and prominence. She carried herself with an air of somebodiness. When Americans, both black and white see her they know they are looking at someone special. At first glance they may not recognize her as an African, but when they do, they are both surprised and impressed. I dare say that most people who come into contact with her want to know more about her and want to spend time in her company. She has special gifts, that much is certain. Though she is from an elite background in Nigeria, she was wise enough to know that it carried no special benefits, social or otherwise in America. At least not with the locals (Americans).

In addition to that, rather than being in the mindset that she was somehow better than many of the people she came in contact with, she instead made them feel better about themselves after having met and talked with her. People of importance as well as those of insignificance would fall all over themselves in attempts to assist this young lady in whatever endeavor she may have been involved in. She had a wonderful way of making people feel welcome. Now that I've spent time in Africa, I can see that it was the positive aspects of her culture that endeared her to her new found friends and acquaintances in America. In Ghana anytime there is a Durbar or official gathering of the Chiefs and the important people in the communities, there is a time when all the visiting dignitaries file by the chiefs, greeting and shaking hands with one another. When I look back through the years at my friend from Nigeria, I see her doing the same thing, going down the line greeting everyone like she is the visiting dignitary and they are the local chiefs and queen mothers.

It all comes back to attitude. A positive attitude and healthy disposition makes one feel better about themselves, and it also makes others feel and act better towards you. A positive attitude, a belief in oneself and one's abilities, a belief in God and a respect for fellow human beings can help one soar like an eagle. *Attitude determines altitude.* If you think you can more than likely you can and you will.

Chapter Five
Save Save Save!

In a consumer society like the United States of America, saving money on a regular basis will be one of your most challenging endeavors. If you want economic independence and financial success you will have to swim against the tide and save in spite of yourself. Unless you are one of the few who happens to be independently wealthy, have a significant trust fund or are backed by a family with plenty of money, you will need to cultivate the habit of saving as much money as you can, as often as you can. My father (May he rest in perfect peace), once told me, *"A made up mind is half the battle and a made up mind is hard to beat!"*

Once you make up your mind to pay cash as you go for all your needs, while sacrificing your wants for a latter day, you'll be in a much stronger position to save on a regular basis. One good reason you'll be able to save is because you won't be spending ten to twenty percent of your wages or

The African Guide To Success And Prosperity In America

earnings on interest payments for things you probably didn't need in the first place. Once you learn to pay cash for the things you need and exercise a fair amount of discipline, you'll be able to squeeze something out of what you earn on a bi-weekly or monthly basis and put it into a regular savings vehicle.

There are plenty of safe places to save money in America. Your house or apartment is not one of them. In Africa, many petty traders don't use the local banking systems for one reason or the other. I've read articles in The Daily Graphic in Ghana where armed robbers have stopped long distance buses and tro tros on the highways and robbed everyone on board. I've also read more than once, where market women have lost several thousand cedis at a time to these armed robbers.

Now I can't say for certain, but I doubt very seriously that these market women are making several thousand cedis a day. If I'm correct and they are not making that much money a day, my next guess is that they are carrying around large sums of money for fear of leaving it at home and taking the chance of it being stolen. In Ghana, the armed robbers quite often carry out their sinful deeds inside people's homes. If the armed robbers didn't think people kept large sums of money at home, I doubt that these home invasions by armed robbers would occur with such frequency.

The African Guide To Success And Prosperity In America

Going to the bank in Ghana can be an ordeal. It will try your patience to say the least. The lines are long and the tellers are few. People easily spend thirty minutes and longer just making simple withdrawals and deposits. The African immigrant to the U.S. will find that the banking system works much more efficiently. The first of the month and pay days can be stressful if one is in a hurry, but for the most part you can go in, do your business and be back out within five to ten minutes. Usually the tellers are professional, polite and respectful. When you show them the same courtesy, it will make life that much more pleasant.

When it comes to where you want to save your money, banks are not your only option. The United States also has an abundance of federally insured credit unions. They operate in a similar manner as banks. Opening a savings or checking account at either institution is an easy and simple transaction. Every time you get paid, you should pay yourself first before you start paying bills, by leaving some of what you've earned in a bank or credit union savings account, or some other type of investment vehicle.

When I was twenty years old I worked for an insurance company selling a product to the public that was two thirds life insurance and one third annuity. Webster's 21st Century Dictionary describes an annuity as, "Annual income

The African Guide To Success And Prosperity In America

brought from an insurance company." The annuity was a savings feature built into a life insurance policy. It was a long term investment feature of the product. We were trained to encourage people to pay themselves first! It was good training and it is based on sound financial principles. The idea is to pay yourself first, before you start paying bills, before you go shopping, before you spend any money at all, pay yourself first. Pay yourself first by taking some off the top and putting it in an investment vehicle like a mutual fund, stock fund, real estate fund or into a long term savings account at the bank or credit union.

The options are many. Most banks and credit unions have departments where people can make direct investments into approved mutual and stock funds right at the bank or credit union. You can also invest in treasury bills and certificates of deposits (CD's) at the credit union or bank. As a matter of fact, many employers give their employees the option of saving a portion of their earnings by investing them in mutual and stock funds through employer sponsored, federally approved financial institutions. You can also hire a personal financial broker to help guide you in setting up your investment portfolio. The point is that in The United States of America, there are systems and institutions in place that will gladly help you when it comes to setting up and even organizing a savings and/or investment program.

The African Guide To Success And Prosperity In America

In my opinion, the home is the least safe place to save significant sums of money. The reasons may or may not be obvious to the reader. For the vast majority of Americans, home invasions by armed robbers isn't much of a threat. Rather than attacking business people and petty traders like they do in Ghana, the home invaders and armed robbers in America usually target drug dealers and criminal types, those who are known to keep large sums of cash stashed at home and other hiding places. For the other 99% or so of the population, armed home invaders are not the problem.

Burglary while one is away from home is a possibility. Few people experience it but it does happen. If you are unlucky enough to have it happen to you, it would be more than a shame for a small time burglar to discover your lifesaving while stealing your other small possessions. Fire is another unfortunate occurrence that can happen to anyone. Again, you wouldn't want your life savings to go up in smoke because you had it hidden beneath your mattress instead of stashing it at the bank. Depending on what part of the country you live in, Tornados, earthquakes and floods do occur. A tornado can rip your building apart and scatter its contents like they were leaves blowing in the wind. Natural disasters occur on a regular basis, even in America.

The African Guide To Success And Prosperity In America

When you save your hard earned cash at a bank or credit union, your money is insured by the federal deposit insurance corporation for banks and a sister organization for credit unions. Your money is insured for an amount of up to $100,000! I know most of us will figure out a good plan for our savings long before we reach the $100,000 mark. The point is that it's backed by the federal government, it's protected and it's safe.

If one is only able to save $100 a month that comes to $1,200 for the year, $6,000 for five years and $12,000 for ten years. That's before interest earnings or other increases to the original principle. If you can save $200 per month it comes to $2,400 a year, $12,000 in five years and $24,000 in ten years! Again, that's before interest or other increases to principle. With a $10,000 bankroll, even in America, a person can start some kind of business and that's without the need of a bank loan. If you already have $10,000 plus interest saved at your local bank you will be in a much stronger position if you have to go to your banker for a loan to start your business. You will also get the loan at a more favorable interest rate.

It all comes down to saving off the top and saving on a regular basis. Paying yourself first. It requires discipline. It requires vision. It requires sacrifice. It requires living within or below ones means. The key is learning how to save, save, save.

The African Guide To Success And Prosperity In America

If you plan to be financially independent and accumulate wealth in America you will have to live below your income, at least for a time, so that you will have disposable income to *save, save, save.* The sacrifice will be well worth the effort and your children will have you to thank for carving out a future of prosperity and comfort for them and their descendants.

Chapter Six
Wages and Occupations

The United States has a federally mandated minimum wage law. This is a minimum wage that is set by the United States Federal Government and as long as you don't work in what is called *the informal sector* in Ghana, you will receive at least the minimum wage. At the time of this writing it is at or above $7.50 per hour. That comes to 290 U.S. dollars a week. Most employers in the U.S. pay bi-weekly, so it would come to $580 per pay period. Federal, state and local taxes are taken out of every worker's paycheck before they are paid. After taxes, a single person with no dependant's making minimum wage will bring home approximately $495 every two weeks. A single person with dependants will be taxed at a lower rate, as would married couples. This means that their take home pay will be greater.

This is a good place to talk about automatic deductions from your paycheck. If you work in a state or for an employer that requires you to join a union, or if you join a union of your own free will, there will be dues taken out of your pay for the privilege of union representation. The dues may be deducted either bi-weekly or monthly, depending on the agreement the union has with your employer. If your employer offers life and health insurance and you take the opportunity to be covered by his plan(s), your premiums will be deducted either bi-weekly or monthly.

Your employer may also allow you to invest in mutual and stock funds through approved and federally regulated financial institutions. Some large firms will even match the amount of money that the employee invests in these funds, up to a specified threshold. It's called *matching funds* and it's one of the very best opportunities that a person can have when it comes to letting money work for you. It's like getting *free money*.

The matching threshold is usually up to six percent. Say you have ten percent of you pre-tax earnings going into the company approved investment fund. Let's say it comes to $100 per pay period. If your employer matches all contributions up to six percent, it means your employer will put $60 into the same fund, or funds you are investing in, under your name and on your behalf. If you only put in six percent of your pre-tax earnings, and that six percent comes to say $60, then your employer will match that six percent and contribute $60 to your account, on your behalf.

Not all employers do matching funds, so if you are blessed to work for one who does, be sure to take full advantage by contributing at least up to the threshold amount. It is a wonderful way to invest and let your money work for you while you work for the company!

Occupations and Positions

A sizable percentage of immigrants come to the United States with inferior educations, training and job skills. Some come as refugees, running from war torn areas and political oppression. Some were poor people in their home countries and were never afforded the opportunity to go to school in the first place. Others couldn't afford the school fees and had to work from the time they were children so that the family could eat every day. Some were able to attend primary school in their home countries but weren't able to go beyond the primary levels. Even those who were able to complete what we in America call high school, many may not have received the kind of quality education that would allow them to function at a competent level in American society.

The African Guide To Success And Prosperity In America

If you are one of the lucky few who have been able to obtain a university degree, you'll have an easier time fitting into the world of institutional work in the U.S. Whatever your station or position is or was when you left your native land, when you reach the shores of The United States of America there will be a hope for a decent life. There are positions and jobs that are available that require a limited amount of training and skill that pay pretty well. I'll mention a few. There will be others that friends, family, neighbors and co-workers will tell you about and how to get them.

Professional Truck Driver

Professional truck driver is the first position I'll talk about. It's commonly referred to as OTR or over the road driver. These over the road truck drivers drive the entire 48 continental U.S. states and into Mexico and Canada. Over the road truck drivers, pretty much live in their trucks! We refer to these tractor trailer trucks as eighteen wheelers, because when they're all counted, that's the actual number of wheels they have. The front part of the truck is like a tractor that pulls a trailer. The trailer

The African Guide To Success And Prosperity In America

is usually between forty eight and fifty six feet in total length.

A large portion of the countries goods move throughout the nation by way of these tractor trailer trucks, on the interstate highways and backroads. The operator will be in perpetual motion driving from one city or town to another picking up and dropping off loads. He or she will drive approximately five hundred miles a day. The more miles the operator logs, the more money they are paid. The pay for OTR is based on a figure that is pegged to the number of actual miles driven. For instance, a new driver fresh out of truck driving school may be hired at the rate of thirty one cents per mile. So if that driver logs five hundred miles a day, it means that they've earned one hundred and fifty five dollars for that day's work.

It's not unusual for the professional, over the road truck driver to spend four to five weeks on the road before returning home. They may only get home a few days each month. Once the driver acquires a few years of driving experience, he or she might get a route that brings them back home every weekend. Some are given what are called dedicated runs that bring them home every few days or so. Like with most jobs in the U.S., seniority plays a part in the type and quality of work one does, as well as the pay they receive for doing it. Pay increases come along with experience and

The African Guide To Success And Prosperity In America

seniority. Instead of the thirty one cents per mile earned just out of truck driving school, the experienced driver may earn thirty seven to forty cents per mile.

To qualify as a professional truck driver you'll need a class A Commercial Drivers License, commonly referred to as a CDL. The class A is the highest form of CDL one can get. It allows one to drive the largest and heaviest of vehicles. Most truck drivers start their careers by going to an approved truck driver training school.

Many of the nation's largest trucking firms operate their own driver training schools. The cost of attending the schools is usually a few thousand dollars. The trucking companies that run the schools will also finance your tuition. This means that when you attend a company sponsored driver training school, the company will finance your tuition cost and will hire you as soon as you successfully complete the driver training course. You'll pay back the cost of attending school to the company that hires you, if they also financed your schooling. They'll spread out the payments over a specified number of months so that it is not too much of a strain on your budget.

The first phase of truck driver training usually takes six to eight weeks to complete. After this first phased is completed you'll be on the road

The African Guide To Success And Prosperity In America

with a professional truck driver who will also be your on the job trainer. This phase will last for another month or two. Once this phase is completed you'll be assigned a rig and given your schedule. This is where the rubber meets the road. From this point going forward you'll be operating as a professional truck driver, driving the forty eight states plus Mexico and Canada.

Professional truck driving is not for everyone. It calls for sacrifice and long days and weeks away from home. On the up side, it's a good way to save money. Driving night and day leaves little time to spend money on anything other than food and drink. Couples can also drive together as a team. Be they husband and wife, girl friend and boyfriend or total strangers, they can share the same truck and duties. While one person drives the other one sleeps and while the other sleeps the other drives. Yes indeed, women in the U.S. are also over the road truck drivers. It's still a non-traditional role for females, so their numbers are relativity few, but still they share the road delivering the nations goods along with their brother truck drivers.

The daily newspapers in most American cities have advertisements in the classified sections for truck drivers, as well as truck driver training schools. The only educational training that one needs before starting one of these schools is a high school diploma or a G.E.D. I talked earlier about the

The African Guide To Success And Prosperity In America

G.E.D., what it is and how to go about getting it. If the immigrant doesn't have a high school diploma that is recognized by the authorities in the U.S. then my best suggestion to them is go and get your G.E.D. as soon as possible.

School Bus Operator

A school bus operator is a driving position that is relatively easy to get. It too requires a CDL, but a class B instead of class A. The difference is the weight allowance of the vehicles that one is allowed to operate. The required driving and written test will also be different. The driving test for the Class A will be in an eighteen wheeler, tractor trailer truck, while the Class B driving test will be conducted in a School bus. The school bus operator will also get a passenger endorsement on their driver's license, allowing them to drive a bus while carrying passengers.

Most school bus companies in the U.S. provide their own training for their newly hired drivers. They'll train you, within thirty days to drive a big orange school bus that is about forty feet in length. Once the training is completed you'll be

The African Guide To Success And Prosperity In America

given a written and driving test by someone licensed by the state. In many cases one of your driving instructors will be the one who will also give you the test. Once you pass the driving and written tests you'll be issued a CDL class B driving license with a passenger endorsement. If a person wants to become a professional truck driver but can't afford the school tuition this is a great way to get a start in the driving profession. You can get a CDL and get it for free by being a school bus driver. Once you've acquired a CDL you'll have numerous opportunities for driving positions.

Once you have your CDL the school bus company will hire and train you to pick up and drop off school children of various ages and backgrounds. You'll be assigned a regular route to drive five days a week, Monday through Friday. You'll pick up the children at designated stops in the early morning and drop them off at their schools. More than likely you'll be off work in the afternoons for several hours, then return before the end of the school day. You'll return to the schools, park outside and when the bell rings signaling the end of the school day, you'll pick up the same children you dropped off in the morning. You'll drop them off in the afternoon at the same places from which you picked them up in the morning.

School bus drivers are normally considered as part time employees. They'll work between

The African Guide To Success And Prosperity In America

twenty five to thirty five hours a week. Because they are considered as part time employees they might not get all the job benefits that a full time employee would expect. The main benefits I'm referring to are life and health insurance. They might get life insurance but probably not health insurance and if they do the premiums may be too high for them to afford. They may also not be offered any kind of employer sponsored retirement accounts. If benefits are important be sure to ask when you interview for the position.

The average pay for a school bus driver ranges between $10 and $15 an hour. Once again it depends on what city and part of the country you are in. Like I mentioned earlier the great benefit of being a school bus driver is the fact that one gets free training for their CDL. Once it's acquired it can be put to use in any number of ways. You can drive for tour bus companies, bus companies at airports, taking passengers to and from their parking lots, and even with long distance bus operators like Greyhound, Jefferson Lines, The Mega Bus and any number of similar bus companies. A CDL class A or class B is a good license to have and it can keep one employed in the U.S.

Certified Nursing Assistant or CNA

Health care occupations are very popular in the United States, especially with the immigrant African community. I would dare to guess that there are more African born medical doctors working in The United States of America and Western Europe than the entire African continent. The reason is not difficult to figure out. They probably earn more in America and Europe in a week than they earn in Africa in a year. It's a sorry state of affairs for the mother continent, that's for sure. The fact that the brain drain of the highly educated, trained, and skilled has left Africa in such a poor and undeveloped condition is heartbreaking, especially when it comes to medical facilities and health care.

Many African immigrants in the U.S. who lack higher education, training and skills still find their way to the health care system and a waiting profession. The certified nursing assistant, commonly referred to as a CNA is one of the more accessible occupations in the healthcare industry.

The African Guide To Success And Prosperity In America

There are many schools and institutes that offer training in Certified Nursing Assistant. The initial training last about ninety days and consist of both theory and practical aspects of health care. CNA's are needed in all areas of health care. They work in hospitals, nursing homes, senior citizen community centers, retirement homes and even in private homes looking after the residents that are in need of assistance.

The duties of the CNA are basic and require only a minimum of training. They change the bed pans (chamber pots) of the infirmed, wash their bodies, assist them to and from different parts of the hospitals and nursing homes, along with a number of additional duties.

The pay can range from $8.50 to over $15.00 an hour. Pay rates vary by region of the country as well as whom you work for. Some CNA's work as live in assistants for the elderly and the infirmed. Some are paid to live in the resident of the client on a twenty four hour basis. Their duties may include cooking and cleaning as needed, as well as grocery shopping and assisting the client in limited ways around the resident. Others will go to the home of the client and work for eight to twelve hours a day as needed.

I have a friend from Cameroon who did this type of work in Minnesota. She would go to the

The African Guide To Success And Prosperity In America

home of her client and stay for twelve hours at a time. When her shift was over, another CNA would show up to relieve her. The client had twenty four care, divided between two people. There are many and diverse positions that the certified nursing assistant can take good advantage of.

Many people that hold CNA certificates return to school for further training. One of the more common courses after the completion of the certified nursing assistant training course is the CMT, or certified medical technician certificate. The CMT is a step above the certified nurse because they're allowed to dispense medication to the patients. They don't give injections, but they are allowed to dispense medication in pill form. The work is a bit less physical and the pay a little higher. Women as well as men work as certified nurse's and certified medical technicians in the U.S. Both positions are usually full time but they have part time positions available as well.

The U.S. population is aging rapidly and there is a continual need for personal in all areas of the healthcare field. One can find work in all areas of the country once they've been certified as a CNA, CMT, LPN, RN, or any number of other occupational areas in the healthcare field. Just like with professional truck driving, you'll find advertising in the classified sections of most daily newspapers listing nursing schools in your area.

Financing will be available and once you complete the course, work should not be hard to find.

LPN and RN

The next logical step up the ladder from CNA and CMT is LPN, or licensed practical nursing. To gain acceptance into the LPN or RN programs you must first complete certain prerequisites. Prerequisites are classes one must take and pass with an above average grade, before being accepted into the LPN and RN programs. Once you've completed the prerequisites, you'll be able to apply to the schools of nursing. Nursing is a very competitive field and they only take the most qualified candidates. Once you are accepted into the nursing program it will take an additional twelve to eighteen months to complete your course work for the LPN program and it will take at least two years to complete the requirements for the RN program.

Degree programs in nursing are available at community colleges as well as at some trade and technical schools. There may be additional board certified training programs in your community that offer nursing training. Starting wages for LPN's can easily go over $13 an hour and top out at over $20

The African Guide To Success And Prosperity In America

per hour. Like for CNA, there are job opportunities throughout the health care system. This is a career that can bring personal satisfaction as well as very good pay.

The Registered Nurse is at the top of the nursing food chain. She's above the CNA, the CMT, and the LPN in education, training, responsibility and pay. An RN in the United States can easily make $70,000 a year and above. It will take more time and effort, as well as sacrifice to become an RN, but in the long run the reward will be well worth the effort. Registered Nursing degrees are usually conferred by colleges and universities. Some of the major hospitals also have in house RN programs.

You'll need a well developed academic mind to deal with the rigors and overcome the obstacles on the way to a degree as an RN. Once again, the degree programs for Registered Nurse are very competitive and they only accept the candidates who make the top grades in the prerequisites. If you like the academic life, are good in math and science, the registered nursing degree may suit you well.

Becoming a certified registered nurse is by no means easy. It poses a major academic challenge, but those who are fit to the task, will have a profession that will provide all their worldly needs and a sizeable chunk of their wants and desires. The need is vast and the field is wide for RN's. The board certified RN will have the world at their beck and call. They are in need and great demand all over America and throughout the world. I stated earlier that once accepted into the training program it will take at least two years to complete the course. The RN is a Bachelor of Science degree and usually takes every bit of four years to complete the entire course requirements. Starting pay is in the neighborhood of $25 an hour and above. There are nurses who have been practicing in the field for a number of years who make a six figure annual income.

Construction Workers

Construction is big business worldwide, including in The United States of America. The work can be challenging and physically difficult. There are days and times when the construction workers are unable to work because of bad weather, be it rain, snow, or just too darn cold. How the weather affects one's ability to work in the construction field will largely depend on what part of the country you settle in. The northern parts of the nation experience more extreme winters, with colder temperatures and snow and ice. On the other hand, the southern regions of the country have it much easier during the winter months. Some of the southern states receive very little to no snow, with temperatures rarely dipping below 32 degrees Fahrenheit. This means that your chances for year round work will be much greater in the south, as compared to the northern areas of the country.

The work may be seasonal, especially in the north, but it is still a lucrative field for employment. The hourly rates of pay for skilled trades can easily top out over $20 per hour, with some skilled trades paying over $30 per hour. With pay rates that high, one who is prudent should be able to manage their affairs, without working fifty weeks out of the year. Working seasonal means you'll have to be a good resource manager. It calls for discipline when it comes to spending. When you are subject to being laid off of your job due to inclement weather or the job has been completed or any number of other reasons, one has to learn to manage their income wisely, even when they are pulling in well over $1,000 per week.

The vast majority of construction workers are skilled laborers. They're carpenters, pipefitters, welders, cement finishers, bricklayers, electricians, roofers and other skilled trades. One category of construction work that pays well but requires little formal training is the general laborer position. The

The African Guide To Success And Prosperity In America

construction industry in the United States is largely controlled by labor unions. The labor unions also set up some of the apprenticeship training programs for the industry. Other groups also run apprenticeship training programs. If one is interested in working in the construction field, he or she would be well advised to seek out a program that offers apprenticeship training for the various skilled positions. The highest skill level in the industry is the journeyman, and to reach that level will take several years. The training is broken into two parts, classroom theory and on the job practical training.

Once you're accepted into a qualified apprenticeship training program, you'll be placed on a work site within a few weeks to begin your on the job training. You'll be paid while you're still in training. For instance, if you're training to become a journeyman painter and the hourly rate of pay for a journeyman painter is $27 per hour, you'll be paid a percentage of that $27 per hour to start out. Over a period of time your rates of pay will rise until you eventually max out at the top pay scale, once you've completed your journeyman's training. If the journeymen rate of pay for the position you're training for is say $26 per hour, and you are paid at half the journeyman rate to start, then your starting rate of pay will be $13 per hour. By the end of your apprenticeship training you'll have become a

The African Guide To Success And Prosperity In America

journeyman and you'll start receiving the top pay for your skill area.

Once a person learns a trade, acquires a profession or a skill, they will be in a position to have more independence that the average worker. That's the beauty of skills and trades. They give one a greater sense of independence. Once you become a journeyman you'll not be totally dependent on the union sending you out on jobs. You'll be in a position to find jobs on your own when the union doesn't have one, or if they don't have the one that you want. The jobs you find on your own will naturally be on a smaller scale, but you'll have more control over where, and for whom you work. If you're a journeyman carpenter you can build a recreation room in the home of a neighbor or friend. If you're a journeyman plumber you can do plumbing work for small businesses as well as for homeowners and real estate companies. You may even decide to become a contractor and hire skilled workers for jobs that you set up and organize.

Construction in the United States is a very big industry and it controls an awful lot of money. It's not always easy getting into. There's an element of racism that will be a challenge for the non-white. Dealing with it will require patience and perseverance. We have another saying that goes like this, "Education is the one thing that they can't take away from you." Once you've learned a thing, be it a skill, a trade or university degree, the knowledge can't be taken away by anyone. You'll be able to use your creative mind to draw benefits from it for the remainder of your natural born life.

Beauticians and Barbers

Beauticians and barbers are occupations that also require training, then licensing by the states. For the female, African hair braiding can be a field unto itself. If all you do is braid hair and add extensions you can make quite a sum of money in the U.S. Doing just one client a day six days a week will pay the bills and then some. Even if you're only braiding hair, many jurisdictions will require a license by the state or other local authorities. The training requirements to become a licensed cosmetologist vary from state to state. Each state sets up its own laws, rules and regulations that govern the licensing and training to become a cosmetologist. Some states will require the student to complete a total of 1200 class room hours, while other states require 1500 class room hours and others still may require the student to complete

The African Guide To Success And Prosperity In America

1800 to 2000 class room hours of study and practice.

The cosmetician (beautician) will be trained in all phases of beauty culture. They'll receive training in hair coloring, hair cutting, manicuring, applying relaxers and permanent waves, neutralizing shampoos, as well as training in all areas of sanitation. You'll be trained in how to keep your brushes, combs, nail files and other instruments and implements clean and sterile so as not to cause or pass on germs, infections or disease. You'll learn plenty of theory as well. Entire chapters will be devoted to the study of anatomy, biology and maybe a bit of chemistry as well.

The average student will take between twelve and thirty six months to complete the entire course. Once you've completed the necessary hours, you'll be required to sit before a state board and be tested in all areas of beauty culture. If and when you pass the state board examination you'll be given your license to practice in the state where you reside.

Beauty culture schools are in just about every major city. Part time as well as full time classes are available. The part time schedule will require the student to attend classes for four to five hours a day, usually Tuesdays through Saturdays. The part time student can take almost twice the amount of time to complete the course as the full time student. For those who need a regular source of income, part time may be your best option. That way you can go to school while at the same time, holding down a part, or full time job. The full time student will attend classes Tuesdays through Saturdays, same as the part time student, but they'll be going eight hours a day and complete the course in about half the time as the part time student.

Many beauticians in The United States earn a very good living. They can easily earn $40,000 a year or more. The cost of basic services in the hair care industry may surprise you. A manicure can set you back $15 to $20 and in some upscale salons even more. To have the hair braided in the traditional African styles can set one back $150 or more. Cosmetology is like most other professions. Many will barely get by, making just enough to pay the bills, with little left for anything else. The ones who take it seriously and strive to be the best in all areas and aspects of hair care will make a lot of money, and some will go on to a degree of fame and fortune in the industry.

For those who are committed to the profession, the hair care industry can be a very exciting place to be. Beauty culture trade shows are held in major cities several times a year. Bonner Brothers host one of the largest in Atlanta, Georgia twice a year. Beauty culture trade shows are also

The African Guide To Success And Prosperity In America

held in New York, Chicago, Las Vegas and Los Angeles, so whatever part of the country you happen to reside in, there will be a show near you. Major hair shows are the places to see and to be seen, but mostly they are the places to get additional high level beauty culture training. The show's host workshops in the various aspects of beauty culture and for the true professional, training will become a constant in their careers. The conventions are of course great places to socialize, network and have great fun. They have high end fashion shows, competitions in style, coloring and cutting and other phases of beauty culture, fabulous parties and live entertainment. The conventions are normally hosted over the weekends, lasting two to three days.

There are always opportunities for the truly talented and motivated in the industry to connect with, and be hired by one of the major hair care product manufacturing companies. You could land a position as a stylist that travels with the big shows, representing one of the major players in the industry like Soft-Sheen Carson or Revlon. You could just as well go into sales for one of the big companies. Some beauty culturist are talented enough and in the right place at the right time, whereby they become the personal stylist, makeup artist or personal beauty consultant to some of entertainments top celebrities. The field is wide open for the professionally trained cosmetologist. It's not difficult for one to open their own salon, but starting out like in any other field, will take patience and perseverance.

The Barber

Like the beautician, the professional barber has a significant role to play in the hair care industry. He or she also has to be trained by the state. I say he or she because there are a few females who stick strictly to barbering. As a matter of fact I'm friends with a female who owns a beauty/barber shop combination. Every time I've paid her a visit, I found her cutting a man's hair. It didn't dawn on me for years that she was a barber and not a beautician. That's in spite of the fact that each time I visit her she's standing behind a barber's chair giving a haircut. It didn't hit me till one day she told me that she'd attended Mrs. McDonald's Barber College.

Mrs. McDonald had been an instructor at a beauty college in my neighborhood and I'd known her for quite a number of years. Maybe the reason it hadn't registered that she was indeed a barber was because all I could usually think about when visiting the shop was how good looking she was.

The African Guide To Success And Prosperity In America

What's said for barbers can also be said for beauticians. Although the vast majority are females, there are quite a number of male beauticians and many of them do quite well. One of my very best friends was a beautician and I'm not so sure how talented he was as a beautician, but I do know the ladies loved to sit in his chair.

The would be barber like the beautician, will be required to accumulate a certain number of classroom hours of training. They'll have to sit before a state licensing board and pass both the practical and written parts of the test. Once they accomplish those task, they'll be given a license to practice in the state. Once he or she receives their license to work they'll be prepared to go out into the world and make a decent living. The newly licensed barber will usually work in a shop alongside other more experienced barbers while paying booth rent to the owner on a weekly or monthly basis. The opportunity is always available to the barber, whether they are new to the game or seasoned professionals, to open their own barber shop. Barbers attend many of the same hair shows as the beauticians and have some of the same opportunities to work for the major hair care manufacturers as the beauticians.

The African Guide To Success And Prosperity In America

Casino Workers

Las Vegas, Nevada is considered by many to be the gambling and entertainment capital of the world! To fully appreciate the full grandeur and magnificence of Las Vegas, you must see it up close and in person. It has to be seen to be believed. Not on TV or in magazines but in person. There are over 5,000 hotel rooms in the MGM Grand Hotel alone! There are more hotel rooms in one hotel in Las Vegas than there are total hotel rooms in many entire cities! In Las Vegas, they've spent over one billion U.S. dollars to build just one hotel/resort/casino. They spend a billion like others spend twenty million.

The top attraction and the main industry in Las Vegas, is gambling. Everything else comes in second. Oh, there are other attractions in Las Vegas. The biggest names in show business crowd the stages of all the major hotels on the strip seven nights a week. She hosts the world's top acts on a six mile strip like you've never seen. Up until the

The African Guide To Success And Prosperity In America

great recession of 2007-2008 Las Vegas, Nevada had been the fastest growing city in America for the previous twenty years! She was hit with a bolo punch by the economic down turn. Especially hard hit was the housing sector. In spite of her recent ill fortune, I would suggest that the adventurous of you take a good long, close look at what she still has to offer.

I lived and worked in Las Vegas for short periods in 1987, 1997, 2004 and have been in and out for extended stays ever since. When I first arrived in 1987 the average wage including tips for a waiter or waitress was around $35,000 a year. The same goes for cocktail waitresses. The average wage for a bartender was $50,000 a year including tips and I read where some of the bartenders at the top resorts and hotels were raking in over $100,000 a year. And that was in 1987!

I make the point to say "including tips," because when one works in the hospitality industry in The United States of America, especially in Las Vegas, Nevada, tips are a major part of one's income. The American people do believe in tipping. From what I've witnessed in Ghana, tipping is not too common. In fact it may be a rarity. I've read and seen a few reports about other nations and cultures the world over, and it seems that they to, in many cases rarely tip. Not so in the U.S. Depending on

The African Guide To Success And Prosperity In America

where you work and how you take care of your customers, you may be able to live on the tips alone.

Las Vegas' hospitality industry offers many options for gainful employment. I've heard of men with Ph.D.'s working as parking lot valet attendants, and making more money running after cars in Vegas then they'd make by working in their Ph.d degree fields. All the hotels hire maids, porters, maintenance men and women, desk clerks, security personal, and any number of other positions. The hotels in Las Vegas tend to pay a higher starting rate than the nations hospitality industry as a whole.

One of the main things that attracted hordes of people to Las Vegas was the fact that a person who didn't have a university degree and was not highly skilled, could still come to Las Vegas and find a job that paid a higher income on average for doing the same type of work as compared to most other cities. As a matter of fact the unskilled workforce in Las Vegas, in many cases live the American Dream. They've obtained a real middle class lifestyle. They've been able to build beautiful homes, drive the latest automobiles and send their children to decent schools.

The African Guide To Success And Prosperity In America

Dealers

Let me not overlook dealers, for they may be the life blood of the state. The dealers are the men and women who control the gambling games. They roll the dice, spin the wheels, deal the cards, pay out the money to the winners, and collect the money from the losers. Most of the professional dealers in Las Vegas start out by learning how to deal while attending one of the many dealer schools in the city and the state. The schools are relativity short in duration. One can learn three games in about ninety days.

After completing the courses you'll receive your certificate and be ready to apply at any number of hotels and casinos. The life of a dealer comes with high levels of stress. In the end, for many, the money makes the stress worth it. As a person gains knowledge and experience as a dealer in Las Vegas, they can progress up the ladder to bigger and better resorts and can actually become quite wealthy.

Las Vegas, Nevada is the gambling and entertainment capital of the world but she is not without rivals. Up state is Reno, her little sister and she to gathers quite a crowd. Many from the Bay Area in California travel to and from Reno for the weekend, like the L.A. crowd that travels to and

The African Guide To Success And Prosperity In America

from Vegas. Atlantic City, New Jersey probably comes in a distant second in total number of hotel rooms as compared to Las Vegas. She sits facing the Atlantic Ocean and has The Boardwalk as a prime attraction. She's got gilt and glitter and a population of fifty million plus within driving distance.

The state of Mississippi has the second largest total number of casinos. Mississippi is a rural state and has hitched her wagon to gambling in a big way. She's got resorts on the gulf coast and throughout the state. As a matter of fact legalized gambling has taken hold in many places throughout America. Casinos have sprung up on Indian Reservations, by the river fronts and in the wide open plains in places as far and wide as Missouri, Kansas, California, Minnesota, Tennessee and other places to numerous to mention. Wherever there is legalized gambling there will be jobs. Entry level jobs, and jobs that require only a minimum amount of training.

Hotel Maids

The position of hotel maid requires little education and not much training. The worker will be responsible for cleaning a set number of rooms each day. They may be required to vacuum the

The African Guide To Success And Prosperity In America

carpets, clean the toilet and bathtub, the sinks and face bowls, take out the trash and properly make the beds. They'll also be required to replace certain items that the guest may have used, like toilet tissue, towels, face cloths, and coffee. Hotel maids may earn minimum wage to slightly above to start. Once hired as a hotel maid, the person may find that the position pays the bills and is suitable for any number of reasons. Or they may decide that after gaining experience and proving over time that they are a reliable and a good worker, to apply for another position within the same hotel.

Most large outfits in the U.S. give their employees the chance to apply for positions within the organization that give them more responsibility and more pay, after they've worked for the company for a set amount of time. Some organizations require their employees to work in the position they are hired in for at least one year, before being eligible to apply for another position within the same company.

Working as a maid for a large hotel may give one the opportunity to be covered by health and life insurance at an affordable cost. The employee can also expect to get an annual paid vacation after working at least one full year. There may be additional benefits like retirement plans and other benefits that the employee can take advantage of.

The African Guide To Success And Prosperity In America

Maintenance/Janitorial Work

Many companies hire maintenance men to take care of basic functions around their buildings. The maintenance man might do light plumbing and electrical work, take out the garbage and other light cleaning duties. The maintenance man can be an all around fix it person, for jobs that don't require an excessive amount of specialized training. There are courses available for maintenance work in most larger cities at trade schools. The applicant will be trained in basic building maintenance techniques and will be job ready in about six months. Average starting pay for maintenance men is around $11 an hour, depending on what part of the country you live in and again, who you work for. Generally speaking, the larger the company you work for, the greater the chance you'll get benefits, as well as the type of benefits you'll receive.

Janitors on the other hand, require little if any formal training. What training they receive will come from the companies that employ them. For the men who become janitors it will be helpful if you can operate a floor buffing machine. Maintaining the condition of tile floors can be a major part of your duties. Huge office complexes as well as hotels and other buildings require the constant upkeep of tile floors. They require sweeping, mopping, waxing and stripping. Additional janitorial duties could include vacuuming carpets, taking out trash, dusting, sweeping floors, and general cleaning duties. There are usually several janitorial companies in most cities that one can make application to for employment. One can also apply for janitorial positions in places like hospitals and factories. The average starting pay should be around $10 an hour, again depending on what part of the country you're in and the size of the firm you work for.

Convenience Stores: 7-11, Quick Trip, SuperAmerica and Others.

Convenience stores are spread all over America. The vast majority of service stations include convenience stores as a part of their operations. The service station in America is where the motoring public purchases gas (fuel) for their automobiles. In America we say gas, in Ghana and other parts of the world they say fuel. When they speak of gas, they are talking about natural gas, in cylinders, used for cooking. As a matter of fact, in Ghana many of the cars used for taxis have been converted to natural gas. When they talk about a gas station they are talking about going to fill up their gas cylinder in the trunk (like the British they call it a boot) of their car.

Back to convenience stores. The fuel pumps are in the lots and the main building is where the clerks are. In America, ninety nine percent of service stations are what we call self serve. That means instead of someone standing there ready to pump your fuel, you instead get out at the pump and do it yourself. Attendants pumping your fuel and collecting your money went out of style in the 1970's. If you have not used a debit or credit card to pay at the pump, you'll have to go inside and pay at the counter. Clerks will be standing behind the counter, waiting to take your money and allowing you to pay for any additional purchases.

Convenience stores are filled with all kind of *convenient* merchandise. You can buy wine, whiskey, beer, cigarettes, soda pop (coke, pepsi, sprite), candy, gum, chips, coffee, tea, milk, pampers, maps, lottery tickets, ice, bottled water, and a hundred and one additional items. The clerks run the convenience store, service stations. One will be the manager and he'll usually have an assistant

The African Guide To Success And Prosperity In America

manager that'll be in charge when he's not there. Along with the manager and assistant managers, there'll be several clerks. Most service station convenience store operations operate around the clock, twenty four hours a day, seven days a week, three hundred and sixty five days a year.

The clerks and managers spend a lot of time behind the counter, ringing up sales. When time allows they move around the store taking inventory, straightening up stock, mopping the floor and doing various duties. Clerks require training. One needs to be very good at counting money and if they don't know the proper way to run a computerized cash register, they'll have to be taught. There are three shifts working at a twenty four hour service station/convenience store. Early morning to afternoon is the first shift. Afternoon or evening to late night is the second shift. Overnight is the third shift. First shift is usually 7AM to 3PM, second shift is 3PM to 11PM and third shift is normally 11PM to 7AM.

Working at convenience stores and service stations come with a degree of danger. The later it gets the greater the possibility of being robbed! The armed robbers usually strike under the cover of darkness. The best advice I can give to you regarding armed robbery in America is not to resist! This applies to working in a service station/convenience store, a neighborhood bar, your

The African Guide To Success And Prosperity In America

own personal business, walking down the street, or working as a teller in a bank. The little money the robber gets, and in most cases it will not even be your money, is not worth your life.

The pay for starting clerks is usually around $10 per hour. If you go into management your pay could increase to $35,000 to $40,000 a year and above. Working with the public puts one into contact with all kinds of people. The United States of America is a very racially, ethnically, and culturally diverse place. You'll deal with red, white, black, brown and yellow people every day of the week. You'll see and deal with people from all income levels, from the very poor to the very rich. They all come to buy fuel and purchase convenience store merchandise.

When you work with the public it pays to have a thick skin. It will work against you if you take things too personal. People will be in a bad mood, they'll be short tempered, they'll be upset over who knows what and seeing you may give them a reason to vent for any number of reasons. In America we say, "The customer is always right!" It's a business philosophy that usually works for the overall good of the business and is usually the right approach.

When we say the customer is always right, it means the customer is given the benefit of the

The African Guide To Success And Prosperity In America

doubt. The customer is the one who is catered to. The employee is the one with the responsibility of extending an olive branch when a misunderstanding develops between the employee (the store), and the customer. Not everyone has the personality, patience, tolerance or understanding to work with the public. Those best suited will need to have a caring, compassionate, and understanding attitude if they really want to gain success from the venture.

Working with the public will make you laugh and it'll make you cry. They'll lift your spirits on a bad day and they'll bring you down on a good day. You'll never know who you'll meet (like the theme song from the movie Car Wash says). You might meet your future husband or wife. You'll probably make new friends. You might meet important people who will be in a good position to affect your life. If you offend the wrong person, you could meet your worst nightmare. The thing about working directly with the public is that it will never be dull. It will be exciting if nothing else.

Chapter Seven

Houses, cars, groceries and helpful things to know.

Most people have heard of *the so-called American dream.* It's an often quoted phrase in the American media culture. When concrete meaning is given to the term, it usually boils down to the concept of home ownership. That's not to say that it doesn't mean different things to different people, but in broad (media) terms, it still comes down to owning a home. Now whether or not wanting to own a home is a uniquely American phenomenon, is a bit questionable.

What I can say is that the path to home ownership in America can be vastly different than home ownership in Africa, as well as in many other parts of the world. In Ghana, the vast majority of home owners build their own homes rather than purchasing homes currently on the market. In

The African Guide To Success And Prosperity In America

addition to building their own homes, they do it with cash on hand or their own resources, rather than depending on home mortgage loans. There is funding, on a short term basis for home building in Ghana, and the banks are now getting into providing home mortgage loans for new home construction. When one can get a home mortgage in Ghana, they are usually for a much shorter term then the ones provided by financial institutions in the United States. The home financing I see advertised in the newspapers in Ghana are for short periods, usually no longer than twenty four months.

The majority of new homeowners in the United States have their homes financed by banks, credit unions, or some kind of mortgage finance company. When I speak of a new home, it does not necessarily mean that they will be the first one or first family to occupy the structure. The infrastructure in the United States was developed decades ago, so there are houses and apartments being bought and sold daily, some of which may have been built fifty years ago, or even longer. Some of these older houses and apartments are in pretty good shape, but others are in need of major repairs.

The average mortgage payment in the U.S. housing market is for a thirty year period. You can have a house built from scratch, or you can buy one on the market that is five, ten, fifteen, twenty or

The African Guide To Success And Prosperity In America

more years old. Either way, if you have it financed like the vast majority of Americans, your mortgage payment will run for about thirty years!

Your mortgage loan comes with a fixed amount of annualized interest built into your monthly payments. The interest rate is determined by your lender and generally speaking, the longer you've had established credit and the better your credit history, the lower will be your interest rate. Interest rates are a major determining factor when it comes to the total amount of your monthly mortgage payments, including the interest you'll end up paying for your house. The highest housing cost in the nation can be found in New York, California, New Jersey and alone the eastern seaboard.

Overall housing cost in the U.S. can vary depending on a number of factors, not the least of which is what city or region one buys in. Housing cost even vary within metropolitan areas, depending on which section of the city you decide to settle in. Some areas will have extremely high housing cost, based on excellent schools, low overall crime rates, well developed infrastructures (roads, bridges, sewage systems, etc.) nearby medical facilities, and what have you. Other areas by converse, will be much cheaper and for the same reasons. They'll lack good schools, have poor services and older infrastructures, and may have a higher crime rate.

The African Guide To Success And Prosperity In America

Poor social and economic factors tend to drive down the value of property and in many older neighborhoods, these are the realities.

This book is about being a success in America. With success, comes risk, especially in business. No pain, no gain. No risk, no reward. The American Dream. When it comes to acquiring the dream you can have your cake and eat it too. Thank God, there are alternative ways and means to acquiring property in America. One way is through County held delinquent tax sales. These sales are held in some American cities and towns once or twice a year. When homeowners fall too far behind in their mortgage payments, their homes are liable to be seized by the mortgage company who extended the loan! If one gets too far in arrears on their property taxes, their house along with all other delinquents, will be put up for auction and sold at a public sale to the highest bidder. This situation presents a golden opportunity for the person with a cash reserve.

People get behind in their property taxes and put themselves in a difficult position for any number of reasons. It could be that the original homeowner has died and the other family members couldn't come together and agree on who would be responsible for the tax payment. Sometimes the tax

The African Guide To Success And Prosperity In America

payments are not paid because of negligence. Other times people are in such a terrible financial condition that they just couldn't afford to pay the bill. The point is, whatever the reason the house is put on the auction block, it's not your fault and if you buy the house you'll have no reason for guilty feelings. We are all responsible for our own individual lives and it pays to live one's life right.

You can go to your county courthouse or go online to find out whether or not they conduct delinquent property tax sales in your area. If they do, the procedures will be outlined and the dates posted. They'll usually post a list of the properties to be auctioned, giving the addresses of the properties, and the dates of the sale. They usually publish a record of the property to be auctioned two weeks to thirty days prior to the auction.

You'll need to do your own thorough research and investigate each piece of property you have an interest in bidding on. One has to be very careful that the property they bid on is the correct property, and the one they had in mind when they did their research. If one is less than diligent, he or she may end up purchasing the empty lot, next door to the lot with the nice two story brick house they thought they were bidding on. On the other hand one may well end up with that nice two story house while paying a fraction of the market value. I personally know people who have used this method to purchase houses for as little as two to three thousand dollars!

Here's the thing. Many of these houses on the cheap may be in poor neighborhoods. The crime rates may be high and the schools may not be up to par. You can buy these properties for your primary residence or you can buy them as an investment and put them up for rent or for sell. You could do whatever repairs are required, bring the property up to code, then rent the property at market rates. If you do, more than likely you'll recoup your investment in about two years, give or take a few months, after that it will be all profit. Or you can do the repairs and a bit of home remodeling and put it up for sale, in which case you'll more than likely double or triple your investment.

There are people who create very good business income using this method to acquire real estate. I know a Nigerian in Kansas City who used this method to buy about eight houses. He did well until he ran into marital problems. That's a story for another time and place. The point is the method works. It doesn't require special degrees or training. One just needs ready cash and if one lives beneath their means, develops a savings plan, and is patient and preservers, they'll have enough personal savings to buy several houses using this method.

The African Guide To Success And Prosperity In America

Another method of operation (M.O) is to cruise certain neighborhoods, looking for empty, unoccupied houses. When you identify several houses that may suit your needs, make a written note listing the addresses and the appearance of each house. Go to City Hall or the County Courthouse and do a title search, or ask one of the clerks how you go about identifying the owners of specific pieces of property. Once you obtain the address or phone number of the property owner you can contact them direct. Some property owners will be looking to sell and some may even be ready to sell at bargain basement prices. You might be the right person at the right place, at the right time.

Once you make contact you'll have the option of making an outright offer to buy. You could offer them anything; whatever you think the property is worth based on your observation. Of course you may not know what condition the house is in without taking a closer look. If the owner is willing to sell for a reasonable amount they shouldn't mind showing you the property, inside and out. Once that takes place you'll be in a better position to make an offer that is fair to the both of you. If the house looks like it's been sitting unattended for some time and the owner seems willing to sell, you could offer them anything. Your first offer could be between $2,000 and $10,000 depending on the neighborhood and the condition of the house.

The African Guide To Success And Prosperity In America

If your cash reserve will not allow you to give the owner what you think the house is worth, you could make them another kind of purchase offer. You could offer to pay the owner a down payment of say, $2,500 and make monthly payments to pay the balance off in twenty four to thirty six months. If you choose this method, it would be advised that you would hire an attorney to draw up a binding agreement on both parties.

I have a friend who amassed a sizeable investment in real estate using precisely this method. He even went a step further by agreeing with the seller that if he didn't complete the payment plan, he would forfeit his interest in the property and the owner would retain the house as well as the payments the buyer has made toward the purchase price. My friend put this incentive in writing. It was a powerful motivator for the seller to make the deal that the buyer wanted and at the buyer's suggested price. My friend was in a strong financial position and there was never any question of him having the money to complete the deals. This method is not a game for gamblers. It is only for those who have resources and are able to fulfill their obligations without doubt and beyond question.

In the United States of America you will have to be a man or a woman of your word. You can't come back later looking for better terms or

The African Guide To Success And Prosperity In America

more time. The U.S. is a different culture and if you don't keep your word, especially in money matters, things could quickly get out of hand. It is a culture largely based on violence and for every American citizen, there are an equal number of guns. Currently there are over three hundred million Americans, so you can do the arithmetic and figure the number of guns for yourself.

There are between 12,000 and 20,000 murders annually in the land of the free and the home of the brave. With the proliferation, and religion of gun ownership in the U.S. it is no wonder the frequency at which people use them on one another. This is just a word to the wise and a warning to those who would try to trick, cheat or swindle. The United States is not the place to play the fool. Some people in The U.S. will react to such tactics in very extreme and hostile ways.

The last thing I'd like to say is this. The real benefit and blessing that comes from during business in real estate using these M.O.'s is the fact that not only will you acquire properties at a fraction of the market value, but you'll also save thousands and tens of thousands of dollars in interest payments!

The African Guide To Success And Prosperity In America

Automobiles!

Some of the same rules for purchasing houses also apply when purchasing automobiles. Interest rates and credit histories are the primary two. When purchasing a new automobile you can expect the payments to stretch out for up to sixty months and sometimes longer. The rate of interest you'll pay your bank, credit union, GMC, or whoever you use to finance the deal will largely be determined by your credit history or lack thereof. If you've worked to establish a good credit record over a prolonged period of time, and have a job that pays pretty well, you'll get a favorable interest rate on your new car loan. Depending on the shape of the economy at the time of purchase, it could even be as low as one percent.

If you have poor credit you'll find it extremely difficult getting financing on a new or late model automobile, if you can get it at all. If you do get financing with poor credit, it will come at a high price. The high interest rate you'll pay based on poor credit will increase the real price of the automobile and in the long run you'll pay a lot more money for the same vehicle.

The African Guide To Success And Prosperity In America

There are car dealers in the U.S. whose specialty is the customer with bad credit. In my hometown we use to call them, We Finance Anyone Dealers. In fact, that's what they called themselves. The we finance anyone people would in fact finance most anyone. Providing they had a job and it looked like they'd stand a fair chance of paying off the loan. The we finance anyone people usually carry an older inventory of autos and the mechanical condition of their autos is not what you'd expect at a major dealer. That being said, they do serve a purpose and there are a lot of people who without their help would not be able to buy a car.

When signing a contract to purchase a new car, truck or any kind of vehicle, the rule of repossession applies in the same way it applies when you purchase a new house. If you get late on, or miss too many payments (usually two or three), the finance company will repossess your automobile. You'll get up early one morning ready to head off to work and your car will be gone! You may think it's stolen and report it to the police. Before long you'll realize it wasn't stolen, but it was repossessed! If you are ever a victim of this unfortunate event the company who financed your car purchase will still expect you to fulfill the terms of the contract. In plain English, you'll still be expected to continue sending in your car note until it is paid in full, whether you are in possession of

The African Guide To Success And Prosperity In America

the car or not. If you refuse, the finance company will take you to court.

There are several alternatives when it comes to purchasing automobiles, even if your credit history is poor or non-existent. You can go on the internet and search sites like craigslist and Cars.com for used as well as new cars. With this option, in most cases you'll need to have cash in hand for the best deals. Private parties sell a lot of autos on these internet sites. In addition to private parties you'll also see car dealers listing autos on these internet sites, giving the same terms and conditions I've already mentioned for those who have little money, and poor or no credit.

By the time you are ready to go car shopping, if you've been applying the rules of the game, you should by then have built up a sizeable cash reserve. By then you will be in position to go to craigslist or wherever, identify a private seller, pay cash for what you want and get a much better deal, while saving all the interest you would have paid to the finance company. The extra added benefit is the fact that you will not have created another monthly bill that prevents you from saving money for your ultimate goal of financial independence and wealth accumulation. *Cash is King,* and the way to go for the wise.

The African Guide To Success And Prosperity In America

Another way to purchase cars for cash and save a bundle is to go to an auto auction. Auto auctions are held on a regular, reoccurring basis in most American cities. Some auto auctions are strictly for licensed dealers only. More and more you can find auto auctions that are open to the general public. You can search the classified sections of your daily newspaper to find out the dates, places and times of the auctions. If you have auto mechanic skills you can turn buying vehicles at auto auctions into a part or full time business. Some of the vehicles will have body damage and some will need mechanical repairs. If you can make any or all the repairs yourself, you'll be able to buy vehicles on the cheap, repair them and put them up for sale at a nice profit. If you just want a car or truck for personal needs, you have the same opportunity to buy cheap, fix and keep.

Just because one gets a vehicle from an auction doesn't mean it is need of repairs. Some are in very good condition. Of course you get what you pay for so the better the condition, the newer the model, the higher the final bid will be. Even if you are the winning bid on a vehicle that's in good condition, it's always wise to change the oil when you buy a used vehicle. Also, you'll need to carefully check the brakes, tires, battery, belts etc. and change as needed. A person can go to most auto auctions and buy a reliable used vehicle for $1,000 or less. Of course you can always spend more. If the

The African Guide To Success And Prosperity In America

car or truck doesn't start or run, you might get it for as little as $150 if you are willing to take the chance.

There are still more ways to buy used cars and trucks. You'll see them parked with for sale signs in the windows as you travel to and from work. They'll also be listed in the classified sections of the daily newspapers. There will be magazines at convenience stores listing cars and trucks for sale. The point is, if you've saved up enough cash, you'll be in a perfect position to buy a vehicle hassle and debt free. Your car may not be as new or as nice as your neighbor, coworker, family member or friends. But you'll also not have their stranglehold of debt choking the economic life out of you. Most people never acquire any wealth because of their tendency for *keeping up with the Joneses*. That's another American saying. Keeping up with the Joneses! It's a sure fire way of getting deep in debt. Keeping up with the Joneses has caused the financial collapse and ruin of many a good man and woman.

If you do like my co-worker Jack, mentioned at the beginning of the book, you'll pay cash for your autos, invest your disposable income while building wealth and living a stress free, debt free life. It is within your reach and within your power.

The African Guide To Success And Prosperity In America

Groceries

If you've never been to The United States or to the western world, one of the many things that will amaze you will be what we call the grocery store, or the supermarket. In Africa, they are simply called markets. They are outdoors with crowds of people and stalls selling life's necessities. Necessities like food, cleaning materials, soaps, gadgets and whatnots. Someone will be selling tomatoes, another yam, another cassava, still someone else will be selling onion, another one selling okra, another one selling eggs and someone else will be selling all the above and then some. In the United States, relativity speaking, there are few outdoor markets, at least, as compared to Africa and under-developed parts of the world.

What we have instead are huge indoor stores and shopping malls! Grocery stores are the places where the majority of the food is bought and sold. Grocery stores like A&P, Kroger, Safeway, Rainbow, Jewels, Albertsons, Hy-Vee, Price Chopper, Winn Dixie and Giant among others. I say you'll be amazed because these grocery stores have aisle after clean and neatly arranged isle of every food item imaginable. Grocery stores are well lit, both inside the stores and outside in the parking lots. The vegetable section is usually close to the entrance. It will be fully stocked with all the fruits and vegetables that Americans are accustomed to eating. Everything, including the fruits and vegetables will be shiny and bright and look almost perfect. On the downside you may not find some of the staples you've grown accustomed to in Africa.

Most traditional grocery stores in the U.S. don't carry items like yam, cassava, the small green peppers, and a few of the more traditional food items found in African markets. On the other hand what these stores lack in specifics, they more than make up for in abundance. They all have frozen food sections with freezer after freezer, stocked with the kinds of food items rarely seen in Africa and when they are seen there, they are at specialty stores catering to the expatriate community. The frozen food section will have several brands with hundreds of individual containers of ice cream, pizzas, cakes, pies, frozen vegetables, TV dinners, quick meals, along with dozens of additional food items and treats.

Most grocery stores have ten to twenty aisles packed with canned goods, packaged goods, soaps, lotions, detergents, hair sprays, oils, brooms, mops, buckets, dishes, cooking oils, palm oil and all kind of household products. In states that have lotteries, you can normally purchase them at the customer service counter at the front of the stores.

The African Guide To Success And Prosperity In America

You can also purchase money orders, pay utility bills, return merchandise and do other business at the customer service counters. After visiting the grocery store there will be no need to visit the market. You'll have everything you need at one place.

The major grocery stores run sale papers every week, listing a variety of items that will be reduced in price for the coming seven day period. A wise thing to do is to get into the habit of picking up the sale papers of your favorite grocery stores every week. If you like bananas, look for the store that has them marked down this week. There's a grocery store in my old neighborhood in Kansas City called ShopRite. ShopRite has big sale signs hanging from the rafters daily. One of the sale signs that hung daily read: bananas twenty nine cents a pound every Thursday. And since I eat a lot of bananas, I made it a point to shop there just about every Thursday. At that time the regular price of bananas was around fifty nine cents a pound, so I saved thirty cents a pound and I usually buy three or four pounds at a time. It may not seem like much and hardly worth the effort, but just forming the habit of looking for sales and being price conscience can save one a bundle over time.

The other technique that saves money at the grocery store is using coupons! The Sunday edition of most daily newspapers in the U.S. comes with

The African Guide To Success And Prosperity In America

dozens of sale papers from dozens of stores of all kinds. The Sunday paper also comes with inserts of several pages containing manufactures coupons. All you do is tear, or cut out the ones you will use and when you go shopping take the coupons along with you.

Let's say you need spray starch, nail polish, coffee and ice cream. You can normally find coupons for these items along with others in the Sunday paper. Maybe your favorite brand of coffee is Folgers. A one pound can could sell for five dollars. The Folgers coupon may offer fifty to seventy five cents off the price of a one pound can or larger. Some stores will even give you double off the face value of the manufacturer's coupon. This means when the coupon says fifty cents off, the store will match it and give you a total of one dollar off the price of the product. If the coupon says one dollar off and the store policy is to double the manufacturing coupon, it means you'll get two dollars off the price of the product. When a person combines the manufacturer's coupon with the already low advertised sales price at the store, you can save a bundle.

There's a few people who've turned using coupons and sales in the U.S. into an art form. We read from time to time in the media of examples of these savvy shoppers. Every now and again we'll read of a shopper who went to the grocery store and

The African Guide To Success And Prosperity In America

came out with two to three hundred dollars worth of products, (sometime even more) while only coughing up six or seven dollars! I've even read where some have come out with baskets full of groceries and instead of paying they were given money back instead! After combining coupons, sales, and rebates, they were all but paid to come there and shop. I admit, these cases are rare but they do indeed exist. One need not be as savvy as these select few, but one can still use the same techniques to their and their families benefit.

I barely mentioned rebates. Rebates are what manufactures sometimes give to the consuming public for buying their products. Listerine mouthwash may cost three dollars and fifty cents for an eighteen ounce bottle. The manufacture may run a coupon in the Sunday paper offering a rebate of three dollars and fifty cents on the same product. This gives the public the opportunity to have the product for free after they fill out and mail in the approved rebate form, and the sales receipt showing you purchased the product within the specified dates on the rebate form. The rebate will also ask you to circle the product on the sales receipt. All it takes is a stamp and a small amount of effort to get your refund in the form of a rebate.

Being successful takes work. Being financially independent takes some sacrifice. There's no magic bullet to financial success. No *one*

The African Guide To Success And Prosperity In America

big thing. Instead, I would argue that there are many small things to financial independence, wealth building and success in America. The good news is, the small things are within your reach. There's a saying, "Do the small things constantly and consistently and the big things will take care of themselves."

WalMart, Target, Aldi's, African and Oriental Markets

Of course there are more options for groceries than the ones previously mentioned. The United States is a nation of over three hundred million people, with a landmass that stretches over three thousand miles (over 4000 km) from east to west and about two thousand miles (over 3000 km) from north to south. In total world population America comes in third behind India and China. She is the third most populous nation on earth. She's a microcosm of the world. Every nation on earth is represented among the American population, or so it seems. She is very diverse in religion, language, speech, color, ideas, culture, and people. So quite naturally there will be options

The African Guide To Success And Prosperity In America

when it comes to food that reflect the world's populations.

I'm sure that many readers are already aware of what we in the U.S call African Markets. Not markets in the traditional African sense, where there are entire areas filled with shops and stalls. The African Market in the U.S. is more on the order of a small grocery store that specializes in African goods. They stock a good quantity of yam, cassava, traditional African foods, along with DVD'S, clothes, cloths, jewelry and other items of special interest.

Other ethnic groups have their markets in the U.S. as well. Most large American cities have grocery stores or markets that cater to the Mexican and Asian communities as well, in the same way the African Markets cater to the African communities. I have a friend in Minnesota who is from Cameroon and another friend who is from Liberia. Both of these women shop at the Asian markets in their respected neighborhoods. The Asians, it turns out, have food stuffs that the African community is familiar with. Variety they say is the spice of life, and one will find plenty of it in the U.S., especially in the larger cities.

We also have what are called discount grocery stores. Being from the Midwest, the one I'm most familiar with is called Aldi's. It's a no

The African Guide To Success And Prosperity In America

frills grocery store with low prices on all its merchandise. The fresh food and frozen food sections will be smaller than the ones in traditional grocery stores. Aldi and other discount grocery stores carry a large selection of generic brand products, so you may not find the major labels and name brands that you'll find in traditional grocery stores. Brand names cost more so this is one reason why the discount grocery stores are able to offer lower prices on their goods. The fact that they don't carry a large inventory of brand names allows them to keep cost down. With brand name merchandise, whether they're clothes, shoes, furniture, food, jewelry, sunglasses or what have you, a certain percentage of the price comes from the name being attached to the product.

I spent a few months in Las Vegas, Nevada in the fall of 2004. I traveled up and down the strip visiting top men's clothing stores and boutiques. I was investigating the quality, price and designer names of men's suits. I won't mention the names but the prices ranged from $500 to $2,200 per suit! These were massed produced suits hanging from the racks! I asked the salesmen at several boutiques and stores if they could tell me the difference between the suit that sells for $500, versus the one that sells for $1,000 or $1,500 or $2,200? Every salesman I ask told me basically the same story. They talked about the quality of the fabric, the thread count, the

The African Guide To Success And Prosperity In America

hand work, the stitching and then they said the name alone can add $500 to the price of the suit!

When it comes to food, the label won't give as much of a sticker shock, but you can believe that it does go into the final price calculations. As for me, I don't see much difference in a can of corn or green beans whether it is a name brand, a generic brand, or no brand can. To me they pretty much all taste the same. After I doctor them up with a little salt and pepper, some onion and green pepper, I really can't tell the difference. So for me, going to Aldi, Save A Lot (another discount grocery), makes sense and saves me money on the food bill. Since eating is something that we all have in common, this is another area where we can save some hard earned money. I forget what wise man coined the phrase, "a penny saved, is a penny earned," but I think it makes plenty of good cents, I mean sense. When you understand how to save money, then you'll have an idea of how to make money.

The final few places I'll mention for grocery shopping are WalMart, Target, Sam's Club, and Costco. These four are the super stores. They are some of the major players in the retail segment of the economy. They now compete with the traditional grocery stores for the consumer dollar. Sam's Club and Costco are membership based operations. This means that you'll have to purchase a membership card to gain the privilege of shopping at these discount giants. The membership cost are somewhere in the neighborhood of fifty dollars, give or take a few dollars either way. These two retail giants sell plenty of merchandise, Costco's even sells in bulk. This includes liquor sales. Anytime I'm at Costco's I always recognize store and bar owners shopping at these places along with the general public.

WalMart and Target don't require any membership dues or cards and they are both open to the general public. There prices are about the same or slightly lower than the traditional grocery stores. I think there true advantage may lie in the fact that they have everything one needs, from groceries, hardware, auto, cleaning, electrical, entertainment, pharmacy, lawn and garden, books and magazines, kitchen wares, a smattering of furniture and just about anything you can think of. They offer a real one stop shopping experience.

Outlet Malls

I've mentioned the fact that America is a consumer driven society. The economy is based around consumption. It's the main driver of the

The African Guide To Success And Prosperity In America

economy. Americans live to shop, or so it seems. We are on a constant buying frenzy. No matter how disciplined one is, no matter how bad one struggles to live a debt free life, we all are in need of certain basic things that will increase life's comfort and make going to work worthwhile. I've talked about shopping for cars, houses and groceries without breaking the bank. I've talked about grocery stores and super stores like WalMart and Target where all your needs (for the most part), can be found under one roof.

The United States does indeed have retail spaces where individual stores and shops abound. We just don't refer to these spaces and places as markets. In days gone by the places to shop were all downtown. In the 1960's generally speaking, things started to change. Housing patterns changed and development shifted away from the urban cores, which are usually in near proximity to the downtown areas. Many people who were in a financial position to move away from the urban core fled like the house was on fire. They dreamed of and moved to the suburbs and when they moved they took the jobs, factories and businesses along with them. Many downtown districts in major cities loss most of their retail trade in the process. This signaled the beginning of the modern day shopping mall.

The African Guide To Success And Prosperity In America

Shopping malls in the U.S. are one, two, or three story complexes lined from one end to the other and from bottom to top, with one retail store after the other. Clothing stores, shoe stores, furniture stores, department stores like Macy's, Jones, Sears, and others fill these huge complexes. Shopping malls can easily contain one, two or even three hundred separate stores. If you get tire of shopping you can go to an area called the food court and have a meal, or a drink and a sandwich prepared by one of several food vendors.

The *outlet mall* is a kind of specialty shopping center. They are usually one story buildings and may or may not contain the square footage or number of stores as the traditional shopping centers. They are oftentimes located on the outskirts of the city or in places that are a bit out of the way. What the outlet mall has to offer is name brand merchandise at discount prices! The travel to and from is worth the effort. They have everything from pots and pans to clothes, shoes, perfumes, bath and body and much more.

The brand names are not just on the merchandise but the entire store may carry such names as Nike, Nunn Bush, Steve Madden, Eddie Bauer, Banana Republic, Polo, Guess, Gap, and a host of addition name brands familiar to the buying public. These outlet malls offer brand and designer name products and merchandise at discounts ranging from twenty to eighty percent off the suggested retail prices. Outlet malls are great places to shop for high value merchandise, knowing that you'll be receiving it for a great price and a huge savings.

In addition to outlet malls there are also major brands that operate their own individual outlet stores. Big designer names like Saks Fifth Avenue, Neiman Marcus and Nordstrom operate outlet stores featuring their brand name merchandise at huge discount prices. These are retailers who handle only the highest quality of merchandise. The merchandise they ship off to their outlet stores may not have sold as quickly as they'd planned, or it could be that the merchandise was left over from the previous season. Some consumers like only the latest fashions and styles and will not buy last season's stuff. I've done plenty of shopping at Nordstrom's outlet, it's called The Rack (one of my favorite stores), and have always been more than satisfied with the quality, style and price of everything I've ever purchased.

We are all uniquely created individuals, with our own individual personalities, insights, understandings and wisdom. As for me, I can't see myself paying seventy five dollars for a nice shirt when I know where to go to get one of similar style

The African Guide To Success And Prosperity In America

and quality for twenty dollars. Neither will I pay one hundred dollars for a pair of shoes when I can travel to one of my favorite outlet stores and get the same shoe or one of equal style, quality and value for half that price. I use to shop at an outlet in Olathe, Kansas just outside of Kansas City. There was a *Floreshine* shoe store at this mall. They had a pair of black and white Floreshines that had been priced at one hundred dollars, marked all the way down to twenty dollars! The shoes fit so well and felt so good that I could almost use them for jogging.

I'm old school and Floreshine was a name that meant something when I was growing up. Needless to say I was thrilled with my purchase. They also had a belt that had previously been priced at one hundred dollars. I got it for ten dollars. Now I must admit I'd never seen a one hundred dollar belt. Whether it had ever actually sold at that price, I can't say for sure. One thing I can say is this. It is the finest belt I've ever purchased. I've had it well over ten years, use it sometime daily and it is in as nice of shape today as the day I brought it.

I'll mention two additional stores that are not outlet stores in the traditional sense, but they carry designer name merchandise at discount prices. One store is called Marshall's and the other is Stein Mart. I'm sure there are many others but these two I know and have spent a considerable amount of

The African Guide To Success And Prosperity In America

money in. On top of the discounted prices, Stein Mart runs regular advertisements offering additional discounts on its merchandise. For instance, they offer what they call red dot discounts. Any merchandise with a red dot gets an additional discount of say forty to fifty percent off the already low price. I recently purchased a couple of very fashionable ladies watches that had sold originally for close to fifty dollars. They were marked down to fifteen dollars and after using my red dot discount coupon, I got them for a grand total of seven dollars and fifty cents each. Now that to me is how one is suppose to shop.

You can be a well dressed man or woman and spend less than one half the amount of money that those around you spend, while looking just as professional and just as good. We all need clothes to put on our backs. We all need plates and bed sheets and any number of other items. When you know where to buy these items, brand spanking new and at huge discounts, then you'll be able to pay cash, have extra disposal income to invest in your 401k, CD's, T-bills, or in your regular savings account at your local bank or credit union.

The African Guide To Success And Prosperity In America

Chapter Eight

Be yourself, while embracing others.

The Bible says, "We are created in His image and after His likeness." So whether you're from Egypt, Jordan, Saudi Arabia, The Philippines, Hong Kong, Sweden, Ecuador, China, Cuba, Russia, Jamaica, India, Cameroon, South Africa, Panama, Mexico, France, Peru, Poland, Iraq, Brazil, Nigeria, England, Guinea-Bissau, St Kitts, Barbados, Senegal, Liberia, Benin or anywhere in between, you are a child of the living and most high God. You have something wonderful to contribute to this thing called life. In this life all human beings will find themselves in positions and situations where they will have to make adjustments in order to get along. They use to say in my neighborhood, you must fit in to get in.

Situations and conditions like employment, schooling, and even life among family members and

The African Guide To Success And Prosperity In America

your community will require you to make adjustments. We have to adjust our attitudes, behaviors, and our ways of thinking based on outward and even inward conditions. This constant need for adjusting to, and adjusting with the environment does not mean that one should lose the essence of who and what they are in order to please those around them, or to be fully accepted and/or integrated into the environment.

If you were born into the world an African, you'll be an African until the day you die! No amount of hair weave, skin bleaching creams, wigs or education will turn you into something God did not create you to be. If you were born an African, you'll die an African. The same can be said for the Chinese, Japanese, Korean, Mexican, Filipina, and even the European. You'll go out of this world with the same racial and ethnic heritage you came in with. Some may think they've come in with a blessing, while others will consider their heritage a curse. In the end, for the most part, it doesn't really matter. The only thing that matters is what you do with what God gave you. Others will never fully accept you until you first accept yourself. Accept even your limitations, then work hard to overcome what you can.

Whatever your racial, religious and ethnic background is, you may as well accept it and embrace it. You certainly can't change it. When you

The African Guide To Success And Prosperity In America

get to America you won't be able to run away from it or hide it, especially if you're Black, or any other non-white person. People will *see* you and they'll respond accordingly. When people first see you they may respond in a positive manner, but likely they'll have a negative response to you at first glance, especially if you are Black. If you respond to the negative by trying to alter your speech, look, acting and thinking to be more in accord with their look, speech, acting and thinking, you may well be able to more fully assimilate into their world but you'll never be fully accepted.

How can one accept one who doesn't accept themselves? How can an intelligent person fully embrace another on the basis of a lie, when they can plainly see that it is a lie. So my humble advice is to be yourself while embracing others. Don't commit the same crimes against others that they commit against you. Don't mistreat others just because you may have a bit more of what this world has to offer than what they've managed to get. Accept yourself. They are not perfect, neither are you.

The bible says that we all come short of the glory of God. It also says that your righteousness is as filthy rags in the presence of God. Learn to embrace others. We can all learn life's lessons from one another. The greater our differences one to the other, the greater the lessons we can learn from each other. The more unalike we are to one another, the greater the opportunity we have to learn something that we didn't previously know.

Africans have rich cultural legacies. Some of these legacies that we honor and are proud of are the beautiful garments and our ways of dressing in traditional attire. The ways that different African women tie the headscarf that lets one know what tribe they represent. Africans have wonderful and delicious ways of preparing food, be it kenke, palava sauce, yam, stews, groundnut soup, okra stew, fufu, red red, or any number of local dishes. They are mouth watering and at the same time many of them are healthy.

Africans have a wealth of religious experiences and traditions, including Christianity, Islam, Hebraism, African traditional religions like Yoruba and many others. The thought, time and energy that African people put into funerals, weddings, and outdooring ceremonies are amazing and wonderful to see and be a part of. In spite of what the western world may think of you, you have a rich and vibrant culture. Don't be too quick to leave it all behind in your race to fit into the western world. If you embrace it, love it, honor it and even cherish the good that the Creator has placed in you, the world will see it reflected in you. They will come to understand and value your cultural heritage and accept you based on you accepting yourself.

The African Guide To Success And Prosperity In America

I can tell by just looking around that a number of Africans who've migrated to America have already learned the lesson. There are Africans in The United States who dress more in the traditional style in America then they ever did while living in Africa. When you come to the western world, share your history with us. Educate us. Some will believe that you have no history, culture or anything else of value to share with anyone. I suggest that you overlook their ignorance. They and we, are all products of the histories and cultures that shaped and formed us. Don't be afraid to be an African just because you are now living in The United States, Europe, China or anywhere else on God's green earth.

The Holy Koran says, "Allah separated men into tribes and families so that they'll know one another." Had He wanted us all to be the same, He'd have made us the same. We don't really begin to learn until we are challenged. When the status quo is in effect, we coast merrily along, but when change enters into the picture we are forced to consider alternatives. When the Black enters into the White world, the initial effect may be disturbing. Like the ripple caused by the pebble or rock thrown into the water. The ripple causes the attention to focus, and then there's an opportunity to learn something. Don't be afraid to be who you are, who God created. Be your Black self if that is who you are, while at the same time accepting and embracing others.

Chapter Nine
American culture and history

Many people don't read! I didn't say that many people don't know how to read, I said they don't read! This is sad, but nevertheless true. Or as some people say, a true fact. If one does not know how to read, they can be forgiven for not reading. For the ones who know how to read and choose not to, it is a crying shame. It's almost a crime, committed against oneself. Obviously, since you are reading this book, you are in neither category.

In The U.S. we have a saying, "Reading is fundamental." Or as the saying goes, fund to mentals! It's a play on words that is most appropriate. Reading expands a person's worldview, their understanding and their mind. In our modern, up to date, sophisticated and technological world, reading is essential to the good life and all that she has to offer. I would suggest to

The African Guide To Success And Prosperity In America

you strongly that independent reading is another key to success. What I mean by independent reading is reading beyond the scope of the classroom. Self motivated reading. Reading for pleasure or reading for research. Reading because you want to read, not because someone forces you to read.

If you're an immigrant, you need to have an intellectual competency as it relates to American culture and history. You need to have accurate information that is not limited to popular cultural sources like cable TV, network news or popular magazines. Read American history that goes beyond the scope of white male domination and the conquering of the Native American. There are plenty of good books available on history written by *other* Americans who've made huge contributions to this great and mighty land. Read books, on, by and about Black Americans.

If you intend to understand this place called America, Black history as told by Black Americans is as good a place as any to start. Read books by and about the Native Americans, who we call Indians, though they do not come from India. There are more Chinese living in San Francisco, California than most places on earth, outside of mainland China. Read their words about living in and contributing to the power, prestige and world renown of The United States of America.

The African Guide To Success And Prosperity In America

The Bible says, "With all thy getting, get first an understanding."America doesn't belong to any one group of people and if she did the only group who could make an honest and rightful claim would be the American Indian. I could suggest to you an entire list of books to read but that may be a bit overwhelming. This is where you'll need to show some personal initiative. Spend some time in one of your local libraries. Search out the subject matter that is of interest to you.

Take your children along and your younger brothers and sisters. Introduce them early and often to reading materials. Develop in your children a thirst for knowledge at a tender age. The Bible says, "Train up a child in the way he should go and when he grows, he won't depart from it." If you read to your children, take them to the libraries and bookstores from the time they enter preschool, they'll have a much easier time academically throughout their school years.

Don't depend on the TV for accurate information as to what is going on in society. What you'll get instead will be opinion masquerading as facts. You'll get plenty of emotional outbursts, suggesting some deep conviction to a matter of great importance. But what you oftentimes won't get is the truth. If you don't develop the habit of independent research and self motivated reading you'll be lost in a sea of falsehood. The one book

The African Guide To Success And Prosperity In America

I'll recommend you get as soon as you finish reading this book is, "A People's History of The United States," by Howard Zinn. I recommend this book because it is very inclusive of Americans from all races, backgrounds and walks of life, rather than being exclusive to the few, the high and mighty at the top.

We in the Black community have a saying, "If you want to hide something put it in a book, they'll never find it!" This is so true, at least as it pertains to far too many of us. I once had a friend tell me in an almost bragging sort of way, "I haven't read an entire book since I left school!" That should be a thing to be ashamed of, something to be hidden from view, not openly bragged about. But this person put it front and center and acted like it was something to be proud of. Don't be counted among the ignorant. Ignorance just means you don't know a thing. In The United States of America there is no reason to remain ignorant about things of consequence. Not in today's modern world. Sources of reliable information are too easy to access.

The public library is your best source for up to date, entertaining and reliable information. Somewhere in The Holy Koran I read, "Read in the name of Allah." That's a powerful statement, however you understand it. To my understanding, it is putting the power and presence of Allah (God) behind, inside, outside and all around the act of

The African Guide To Success And Prosperity In America

reading. Don't sit in a dark room if you have a light and all you have to do is flip the switch. Reading is like flipping the switch that turns on the light that activates your mind and brings it to a higher level of understanding.

Chapter Ten

Giving back, the final key to success.

God's children have to be kind to one another and treat each other right. We have a saying that goes like this, "The same people you meet going up, you'll meet the same ones coming down." The message is clear. Be careful how you treat people while you are climbing the ladder to success. As you gain financial independence and success be careful that you don't become too arrogant. You can be successful and still be kind and decent to ordinary people. Oprah Winfrey is the richest black woman in America and until the end of 2012 when a Nigerian oil tycoon beat her out, she was the richest black woman in the world. Her net worth is well over one billion dollars! She is not only the richest black woman in America she is one of the riches people in America period.

Forbes use to publish a list of the 400 wealthiest people in America. I can remember when I was in my twenties, how proud I'd be when I'd

The African Guide To Success And Prosperity In America

see the name of John H. Johnson listed among this elite group of Americans. For those who don't know the name, John H. Johnson was the founder and publisher of Ebony and Jet magazines. He produced TV shows, The Ebony Fashion Fair (the largest traveling fashion show in the world), and a host of other subsidiary business enterprises. This was a Black Man in America who was not just one of the richest black people in America, but he was one of the riches people in America, period. I can't remember his ranking among the top 400, but even if he came in at 398 or 399 that would have meant that out of a population at the time of over 200 million people, only 398 or 399 people would have exceeded John H. Johnson in total wealth!

He's passed on now and is with the ancestors, but he wrote an autobiography that is well worth the time it takes to read it. He was a principled man, with a high sense of morality and a well defined character. John H. Johnson set high standards for himself and he expected no less from others.

Oprah Winfrey is the modern day John H. Johnson. The new jack media mogul. I'd like to share my personal observations of Ms Winfrey. I've watched her win over and even mesmerize audiences since 1984. I was visiting a cousin in Chicago at the time and Oprah's show A.M. Chicago was in its first year. She had yet to go

The African Guide To Success And Prosperity In America

nationwide. She was syndicated her second year on the air and went coast to coast. She could be seen in major markets all over America by 1985! I must admit that the thing that most impresses me about Oprah didn't hit me until I'd watched her in action for years. Oprah's star rose and she gained more and more prominence with each passing year. She's hosted, interviewed and sat and talked with all the major players and big names in entertainment, sports, and even politics. When these celebrities sit on her stage, it doesn't matter how big their star is it doesn't outshine the Queen's.

Now here's the thing about Oprah that so touches my heart and makes me so love the human being she is. As big, talented, powerful, successful and influential as Oprah is, when these stars and celebrities grace her stage, Oprah is as excited as her audience! Her ego doesn't get in the way of her showing her natural excitement. She's not so caught up in herself that she can't see and admire and appreciate the talents and gifts of others.

A tiny bit of success is all it takes for some of us to start feeling that somehow we are better than those around us. We want others to recognize all that we have done and are doing. Sometimes we act like they should be thankful that they even know us. Some of us get so caught up in our own personal accomplishments that we seldom if ever take the time to give an honest compliment to those around

The African Guide To Success And Prosperity In America

us who are doing good and positive things. Then we turn around and take all the credit for our success by letting the world know how hard we worked and that we deserve it, as though no one helped us at all.

Thank God for Oprah Winfrey, for she is not that kind of a person. I truly believe one of her major keys to the huge success over the twenty five year history of The Oprah Winfrey Show, is due to her wonderful nature and humble spirit that allows her to make her guest feel the same kind of love and excitement from her that they receive from her audience.

Oprah, like many celebrities, gives a lot back to people in need. Michael Jackson was of the same spirit when it came to giving back and supporting the less fortunate in the community and even across the globe. From what I've seen and read down through the years, many of the newly rich do the same thing. When I say newly rich I mean those who've risen up based on their talents, especially those in the sports and entertainment worlds. The media does indeed report on their good works. Maybe not enough but if you are one who pays attention, you'll see where so and so has a foundation addressing the needs of one underprivileged community or another. Some in society may look down on the rappers, but even they have their foundations and charities, spreading the love around.

The African Guide To Success And Prosperity In America

The last key to success is giving back! No human being does anything of great consequence or importance totally on their own. Everyone has been helped by someone or someone(s) in a special way at some point in their lives. The proper and right thing to do is to acknowledge and give credit to the ones who've done good and made a difference in your life. If you don't get the chance to tell them, then tell others about them. Let the world know.

People sometimes die before we have an opportunity to thank them. Sometimes we don't even realize we need to thank them until it is too late. I'd like to take this opportunity to thank Reverend Rucker, a Baptist Minister from Kansas City, Missouri whom my late father suggested I have a talk with years ago. He has been with the ancestors for twenty years or so and I never got the opportunity to thank him in person. He took time out of his life to counsel and help a stranger in need (me) and touched my life in a special way. It was a one-time meeting but it made a difference in my life and I'll never forget it or him. May Allah be pleased with Reverend Rucker. Even if they've passed on you can still thank them by telling others about them and passing the love around.

Help somebody! Help them with a word, a deed, some financing, some know how, or whatever way God puts on your heart to be of service. When you make it a point to help those around you, be

The African Guide To Success And Prosperity In America

they family, friends or strangers, I believe God will bless you even more.

I remember listening to a speech made by Dr Martin Luther King after receiving The Nobel Peace Prize in Oslo, Norway. He spoke of being on the mountain top in Norway but of the need to go back to the valley! He talked about the least of these being in the valleys of Mississippi, Alabama, Georgia and the American south and having no way out. He talked about black people facing brutality, hunger, poverty, discrimination, and suffering all around, and how it was his duty to go back to the valley to see about the least of these, God's people.

We can all learn by listening to the wise words of Dr King and others. For those of us who are Christians by faith, Jesus didn't come into the world to take, he came to give. He didn't spend much time with the rich and powerful, he hung out with the down and out. He gave sight to the blind, hearing to the deaf, food to the hungry and forgiveness and salvation to us all. So as we use right guidance to make personal and family progress in the world, let's not forget to give something in return for God's blessing us. Give something of value to the less fortunate among us.

The African Guide To Success And Prosperity In America

In conclusion, if this book has been of any value to you I ask that you share it with and recommend it to others. Give it out as gifts to those you feel will take the time to read it.

May your best dreams become reality!

The End

The African Guide To Success And Prosperity In America

Back cover of African Guide to Success in America

This book is written as a guide for creating personal wealth in The United States of America. This book will show you how to make money, how to keep the money you make and how to let the money you make work for you. By the time you finish reading this book, you'll be well on your way to financial independence and wealth accumulation. If you put the strategies, practices, and modus operandi into practice, you'll create the kind of wealth and blaze a trail that can be passed down and followed through the generations by your family. This is not a get rich quick scheme. It is a practical guide to financial independence and wealth creation that can be utilized by any and all.

www.ingramcontent.com/pod-product-compliance
Lightning Source LLC
Chambersburg PA
CBHW070144230526
45471CB00002B/506